ABBEYS AND MONASTERIES

Abbeys and Monasteries

Text and Photography by
Derry Brabbs

WEIDENFELD & NICOLSON
LONDON

First published in Great Britain in 1999 by Weidenfeld & Nicolson

ISBN 0 297 824953

Designed by Nigel Soper
Edited by Tamsin Shelton
Printed and Bound in Italy

ENDPAPERS: PETERBOROUGH CATHEDRAL
HALF TITLE: THORNTON ABBEY
TITLE PAGE: TINTERN ABBEY

Weidenfeld & Nicolson
The Orion Publishing Group
Orion House
5 Upper St Martin's Lane
London WC2H 9EA

CONTENTS

Preface

MONASTICISM HAS ENDOWED BRITAIN with a rich architectural legacy, represented by awe-inspiring medieval cathedrals, majestic ruined abbeys and numerous parish churches salvaged from the wreckage of Henry VIII's Dissolution of the monasteries in 1536. When one stands amid the splendour of a great abbey church, surrounded by soaring stone columns lit by diffused colour from rows of elegant painted glass windows, one does not need to adhere to any particular faith to savour to the full the unique atmosphere created by love and devotion so many centuries ago.

Some of the most beautiful areas of our countryside are graced by ruined monasteries. While many are sadly reduced to no more than forlorn fragments, others stand proudly as roofless shells, their continued defiance of the elements a testament to the stonemason's skill. In appreciation of those who left us such an inspirational collection, I have endeavoured to assemble a portfolio of photographs that portrays the spirit and atmosphere that lingers on in our abbeys and monasteries.

The accompanying text briefly outlines the history of each monastic order and describes their principal sites. In writing this text, I have deliberately avoided the use of too much architectural jargon, as I believe I am not alone in being unable to remember the difference between crockets and spandrels. Cathedrals and churches are still places of worship and in many cases remain largely unaltered since they were built. The order of service, congregational seating and electric lighting are often the only noticeable changes inside. Unfortunately, however, the deteriorating fabric of many city centre religious buildings, caused by a combination of age and air-borne pollution, has resulted in many being almost permanently encased in scaffolding while essential repairs are effected.

Conservation bodies such as English Heritage have recognized the immense historical and archaeological value of monastic sites and have turned many of them into premier tourist attractions, thereby stimulating a public awareness and interest to be carried onwards through future generations. The contents of this book represent a personal choice and are in no way intended as a comprehensive guide, but in making my selections I have endeavoured to include a cross-section that perfectly represents the very essence of Britain's remarkable monastic heritage.

LINDISFARNE PRIORY,
NORTHUMBERLAND
Seemingly impervious to the sun's warming rays, mists from the North Sea frequently linger well into the day over Holy Island, long after full visibility has been restored on the mainland. The grey shroud which obliterates all traces of twentieth-century surroundings endows one of Britain's most atmospheric religious sites with an even greater air of mystique.

St Aidan

The intensely moving modern statue of St Aidan bearing the flame of Christianity stands in Lindisfarne's churchyard midway between the thirteenth-century parish church of St Mary the Virgin and the red sandstone ruins of the medieval priory, built over the site of the island's first monastery, established by Aidan in 635 at the behest of Northumbria's Christian king, Oswald.

Two years earlier, Oswald had gained the crown by defeating pagan King Penda in a dramatic battle fought on Hadrian's Wall. Oswald's forces were significantly outnumbered, but after a session of prayer beneath a large wooden cross that had travelled with Oswald, the result was never in doubt. Having been brought up and educated on the island of Iona, the site of St Columba's influential monastery, Oswald asked Columba to send a missionary who might help to convert Northumbria to Christianity. The first mission failed, but then Aidan took up the challenge and eventually settled on Lindisfarne with twelve monks.

His arrival heralded a golden age of Celtic Christianity in the north. From Lindisfarne itself (see p. 58) came the illuminated Gospels, their pages alive with intricate decoration and colour, while further south at Jarrow the Venerable Bede produced his remarkable work, *The Ecclesiastical History of the English People*.

INTRODUCTION

THE FIRST MONKS WERE CHRISTIANS who removed themselves from society to the Egyptian desert to endure privations and hardship as hermits – the word 'monk' is derived from the Greek 'monos', meaning 'solitary' or 'alone'. Primitive monasteries were established when hermits and their disciples formed into small groups, gradually learning to share the benefits of communal living and worship. St Basil and St Benedict were two early influences on the collective approach to religion, encouraging people to accept that pursuing a solitary course of self-denial and hardship was entirely selfish.

Christianity came to Britain with the Roman occupation, but when the empire crumbled during the fifth century and the legions withdrew, heathen settlers from northern Europe flooded into England, forcing the faith westwards to Wales, Cornwall and parts of Scotland. Even before the Roman departure from mainland Britain, St Ninian had established a small monastic house at Whithorn in Galloway towards the end of the fourth century. Ireland had also became a centre of Christian activity, with St Patrick, who became the country's patron saint, being one of those at the forefront.

Although monks from all those early Celtic communities attempted to convert the Saxons, Angles and Jutes who had spread throughout England, the country remained in the grip of paganism. A period known as the Dark Ages settled over the country, until St Columba's missionaries from the island of Iona began to make inroads into the pagan north. In 597, the same year that Columba died, St Augustine carried the Christian message from Rome to the people of Kent and southern England.

Pope Gregory still regarded Britain as a province of Rome and, as such, he felt it could not be allowed to remain outside the Christian fold. Realizing that each region was in effect a separate kingdom, he briefed Augustine to target the rulers and their immediate families in the hope that their conversion would encourage the population to follow by example.

Aware that King Ethelbert of Kent was married to a Frankish princess who was already a practising Christian, Augustine and his entourage began their crusade in Canterbury. Within ten years, Kent, Essex and London had accepted the Christian faith, and many new monasteries were created out of derelict churches scattered around the countryside. Although significant progress was made, the pace had been slower than anticipated, not only through pagan reluctance to acknowledge Christianity but also because of disagreements with the Celtic movement, which had become firmly established in northern England, over many of the Roman Church's fundamental principles of how religious matters should be conducted.

King Oswald of Northumbria had been converted and installed Aidan and his missionaries on Lindisfarne in 635, but it was a later Northumbrian king, Oswy, who brought matters to a head between the Celtic and Roman doctrines. As his wife came from Kent, their differing interpretations of worship and dates on the calendar caused conflict and confusion. Oswy decided that matters had to be resolved and called the Great Synod of Whitby in 664 where both sides argued the merits of their respective cases.

Disagreements revolved around the calculation of the date of Easter and the seemingly trivial matter of how a monk should be tonsured, but at the heart of the debate was the basic principle of organization. The Celts believed in a less formal, liberal approach towards monastic life, accepting that monks could roam away from the monastery to preach, while the Benedictine Romans demanded absolute authority and conformity within a community.

The eloquence of Abbot Wilfred from Ripon swayed the decision in favour of the Roman religion. Reactions from the Celtic faction varied from total acceptance and compliance to a darkly muttering retreat back to Scotland. Monasteries were reorganized under the Rule of St Benedict, and English monasticism entered the golden age of the eighth century, highlighted by the remarkable writings of the Venerable Bede from Jarrow, the production of illuminated manuscripts such as the Lindisfarne Gospels and the monasteries' position as centres of learning – St Augustine's in Canterbury attracted scholars from all over the country.

That period of growth and advancement ground to a shuddering halt when the Viking raids began in 793; at first they only affected the north and east coasts but gradually they spread inland. Monasteries represented soft targets and were an obvious source of ready plunder, and many suffered repeated attacks over several decades until the monks had no option but to abandon them for good. Quite a large number of religious houses continued to serve the population, however, even though the monks had fled. Groups of clergy, or canons, occupied the vacated buildings but did not adhere strictly to the Rule of St Benedict.

During the first decades of the tenth century, renewed interest in monasticism on the Continent filtered through to England. The appointment of Dunstan as Abbot of Canterbury in 940 heralded a revival that reintroduced Benedictine monks into all the major abbeys, where in some cases the resident canons had to be forcibly ejected.

In 970, under the auspices of Wessex's King Edgar, Dunstan met with other leading abbots and together they drafted a document known as the 'Regularis Concordia', which sought to standardize the structure of daily behaviour and worship throughout English monasteries. Much greater emphasis was placed on the ceremonial and ritual aspects of services, ensuring that formal worship was at all times the main consideration.

The Norman Conquest of 1066 brought dramatic changes to monastic life, gradually sweeping away most of the old buildings and replacing the Saxon abbeys, many of which had been made of wood, with new, elaborate stone churches. Chief architect of the Norman takeover was an Italian monk named Lanfranc, who was installed as Archbishop of Canterbury by William in 1070. By the time of his death in 1089, he had revolutionized the English monastic scene.

Normandy was a great centre of Benedictinism and the new regime sought to banish the English version, which had become normal practice through the Regularis Concordia. As might be expected, a deep feeling of resentment accompanied these changes, as most abbeys also had a French abbot imposed on them. The attendant language and cultural differences made the early post-Conquest years a difficult period for the English monasteries.

The last decades of the eleventh century saw numerous building projects get under way, including the majestic Romanesque church at Durham, but it was the following century that really launched a new era in monastic development. In addition to the churches and cathedrals being constructed on existing sites, new foundations were rapidly established by Norman barons on lands given to them by William as reward for their contribution to the Conquest.

Southern churches were often constructed from Caen stone shipped over the Channel, while those in other regions were built from locally quarried limestone or sandstone. Limited technical resources meant that the cutting of large stone blocks was a long and laborious process, so their use was restricted to cornerstones, windows and doors. The building season

ELY PAINTED CEILING

The majority of medieval cathedral churches were built with stone vaulted roofs, but occasionally timber was used. This was often for reasons of architectural necessity rather than aesthetic considerations, so that high-walled naves would not be subjected to an additional burden. Many East Anglian parish churches made a feature of their hammer-beam roofs, but in Ely's case (see p. 40) it was decided to panel over the purely functional timbers during major nineteenth-century restoration work.

Obscuring the network of beams merely replaced one eyesore with another — a drab expanse of plain wood that sat uneasily between the majestic soaring piers of the twelfth-century nave. The painted decoration was conceived by a dedicated local amateur artist named Le Strange, who traced out the designs on huge sheets of paper before transferring their outlines on to the ceiling. Unfortunately, he died after completing only three panels, and the remainder were finished by a professional artist friend, Gambier Parry.

Much of the work is devoted to biblical scenes from the Old Testament, with the Nativity and Christ in Glory appearing only towards the eastern end. While it maybe lacks the raw impact of Peterborough's original medieval painted nave (see p. 68), the stunning Pre-Raphaelite interpretation of the figures depicted on Ely's ceiling is still a sight to behold.

extended from March to October, which allowed for a period of natural settlement as foundations were generally very shallow, and to extend the height of walls too far in one session would have been courting disaster.

Those who built the big cathedral churches possessed extraordinary skill and bravery: the masons relied on drawings, with perhaps a model and a plumbline as their only technical aids. There were several notable occasions when it all went terribly wrong — Winchester, Gloucester and Ely were just three cathedrals whose towers simply collapsed during the twelfth century.

The majority of monasteries were built following the same pattern. The church was always the most dominant feature, but the desire to build the largest and most impressive place of worship possible often left even the better endowed establishments deep in debt, a predicament from which some of them never recovered. The church would occupy the northern part of the site, acting as a giant windbreak for the domestic buildings grouped around a cloister to the south in order to catch the best light and sunshine, an important factor when such a large proportion of the monks' work was conducted around the cloister.

Despite there being no apparent recruitment policy in respect of class, those joining a monastery were expected to bring with them a donation of money, land or some other form of endowment. This had the effect that most abbeys and priories were populated by people from the wealthier sectors of society, as was particularly the case with nunneries. Women from noble families generally had two options in life, and if the course of marriage and child-rearing was not followed, dedicating themselves to God's service was the likely alternative.

A monk's life was dominated by the timetable of services in the church as laid down in the Rule of St Benedict, a daily round that began with matins somewhere around 2 a.m. That early morning vigil was attended by a circator, whose role was to walk round the church carrying a lantern to check that none of his brothers had inadvertently nodded off, not an easy task when faces were obscured by deep cowls. One puzzling aspect of that first period of worship concerns its actual timing and who decided when it really was two o'clock in the morning. Telling the time by the position of the stars was one method, using a water clock was another, but the accuracy of both must have been open to question. And besides, who ensured that the person whose job it was to rouse others was himself awake?

Periods of worship were interspersed with other activities, mostly centred around the cloister where monks spent hours copying and illustrating manuscripts, many of which were colourfully illuminated with extraordinary skill. The middle of the twelfth century is widely regarded as the period when this art form reached its peak, and some of the work produced during that time in English monasteries is acknowledged as the finest in Europe.

Declining standards of discipline and behaviour in many monasteries led to the establishment of orders such as the Cistercians, founded by reforming groups who sought a return to the strict regime demanded by St Benedict. They shunned populated areas and chose isolated locations in which to build monasteries and churches of architectural austerity where decoration was kept to a minimum, although, in time, even the Cistercians relaxed that approach and some of their later churches were transformed by the elegance and beauty that represented Early English Gothic.

Monasticism and church building flourished during the twelfth and thirteenth centuries, but further progress was cruelly halted by the Black Death, which devastated Europe during the mid-fourteenth century. It reduced Britain's population by about a third, and in its indiscriminate cull, the monastic communities were seriously affected.

Monastic life would never fully recover from that onslaught, especially as so many lay workers had died and their places in the fields and workshops remained unfilled. This labour shortage had grave implications for the monasteries' economic stability. As they were unable to generate sufficient income through their own farming enterprises, many monasteries resorted to letting out property, thereafter becoming no more than glorified landlords, constantly embroiled in rent collection and contractual disputes instead of devoting time to religious pursuits.

Evidence of falling behavioural standards throughout the Benedictine monasteries was further indicated by the introduction of holiday retreats, often created from one of a monastery's manors, where monks could take time off from their duties, and by the fact that monks and nuns received small salaries during the fifteenth century, despite their vows of personal poverty.

BISHOP'S CHANTRY CHAPEL
Winchester Cathedral (see p. 28) is renowned for its impressive collection of chantry chapels, each one a miniature masterpiece of ecclesiastical architecture. William Waynflete's is one of six dedicated to past bishops spanning a period of nearly two centuries, from William of Edington (1345–66) through to Stephen Gardiner (1531–55).

Prior to his appointment as bishop in 1447, Waynflete had been provost of Eton College for five years and was responsible for the foundation of Magdalen College in Oxford. He now lies permanently resplendent in full regalia next to the St Swithun monument on the north side of the cathedral's retrochoir.

The presence of chantry chapels in medieval churches can be visually distracting. They were often built in an architectural style associated with a much later period than their immediate surroundings and, as they were endowed by people of wealth and power, they were there to be noticed. Chantries were a valuable source of revenue, since the benefactors paid handsomely for prayers to be said for their souls long after death. Waynflete's chantry exhibits considerable restraint compared to those of his neighbours – Cardinal Beaufort's lavish Perpendicular edifice and Bishop Gardiner's concoction of Gothic and Renaissance both look somewhat out of place amid Early English elegance.

The Dissolution of the monasteries began in quite a civilized fashion with a parliamentary bill that merely sought the suppression of those smaller monasteries with an annual income of less than £200. The Suppression Act of 1536 was passed without question, and as many of the larger abbeys were represented by abbots in Parliament, suspicions were obviously not aroused at that stage. The process was scrupulously fair, with monks either being pensioned off or found places in larger foundations, but the Crown took possession of all valuables, bells and roofing lead.

A rebellion against Henry VIII's policy flared up in northern England. Called the 'Pilgrimage of Grace', it sought to reverse the closures and reinstate monks and nuns. Although ostensibly a protest solely against the suppressions, it was fuelled by an underlying current of social unrest. Henry was ruthless in his treatment of the rebels and many ended up dangling from an executioner's rope.

During 1537, the screw gradually tightened and pressure was brought to bear on some of the larger houses, even though they were excluded from the terms of the original Act. A series of voluntary surrenders began to take place, often under conditions of emotional blackmail. The abbots' fear was that if the generous terms of settlement were not accepted when offered by Henry's Commissioners, they might be reduced or withdrawn altogether, and as the future looked so uncertain, it was deemed better to have at least some financial security.

One by one the monasteries succumbed and the royal coffers bulged with their treasures, while Henry's army was equipped with new cannon cast from melted-down church bells and the soldiers' muskets loaded with lead shot from dismantled abbey roofs. By 1540 it was all over and England's great monastic tradition was finished. Scottish abbeys lingered on far longer, as they were not subject to the Dissolution; their fate was to be sealed by the Reformation of 1560.

Over four and a half centuries have elapsed since Henry VIII brought the monastic era to an end, but we are still blessed with the most glorious reminders through our great cathedrals and the scores of ruined abbeys that now form such an integral part of our landscape and look as though they will stand for at least another few hundred years.

Map showing the location of abbeys and monasteries featured in this book.

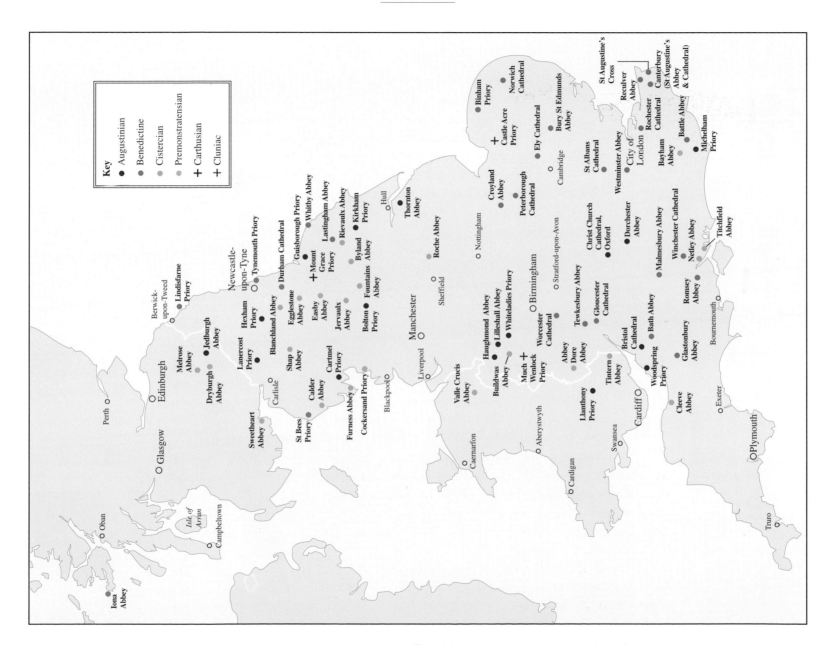

Key
● Augustinian
● Benedictine
● Cistercian
● Premonstratensian
✛ Carthusian
✛ Cluniac

St Augustine's Cross
Reculver Abbey
Canterbury (St Augustine's Abbey & Cathedral)
Rochester Cathedral
Battle Abbey
Michelham Priory
Bayham Abbey
City of London
Westminster Abbey
St Albans Cathedral
Norwich Cathedral
Binham Priory
Bury St Edmunds Abbey
Castle Acre Priory
Ely Cathedral
Cambridge
Peterborough Cathedral
Croyland Abbey
Christ Church Cathedral, Oxford
Dorchester Abbey
Winchester Cathedral
Netley Abbey
Malmesbury Abbey
Romsey Abbey
Titchfield Abbey
Bournemouth
Nottingham
Sheffield
Roche Abbey
Stratford-upon-Avon
Birmingham
Tewkesbury Abbey
Gloucester Cathedral
Worcester Cathedral
Bath Abbey
Bristol Cathedral
Woodspring Priory
Glastonbury Abbey
Cleeve Abbey
Exeter
Plymouth
Truro
Hull
Thornton Abbey
Whitby Abbey
Lastingham Abbey
Kirkham Priory
Rievaulx Abbey
Byland Abbey
Guisborough Priory
Mount Grace Priory
Fountains Abbey
Bolton Priory
Manchester
Liverpool
Blackpool
Jervaulx Abbey
Easby Abbey
Egglestone Abbey
Shap Abbey
Cartmel Priory
Furness Abbey
Cockersand Priory
Calder Abbey
St Bees Priory
Carlisle
Dryburgh Abbey
Melrose Abbey
Jedburgh Abbey
Lanercost Priory
Hexham Priory
Blanchland Abbey
Durham Cathedral
Tynemouth Priory
Newcastle-upon-Tyne
Lindisfarne Priory
Berwick-upon-Tweed
Sweetheart Abbey
Edinburgh
Perth
Glasgow
Oban
Isle of Arran
Campbeltown
Iona Abbey
Haughmond Abbey
Lilleshall Abbey
Whiteladies Priory
Buildwas Abbey
Much Wenlock Priory
Valle Crucis Abbey
Dore Abbey
Tintern Abbey
Llanthony Priory
Cardiff
Swansea
Aberystwyth
Caernarfon
Cardigan

THE BENEDICTINES

CANTERBURY

Cathedral cities are currently experiencing a resurgence of tourism, the modern equivalent of the ancient pilgrimage, although many of today's travellers seem more attracted by the shrine of St McDonald than stunning architecture and reminders of the medieval saints.

Twentieth-century development and a pronounced increase in traffic have tended to dull the appeal of these historic places, especially when beautiful religious buildings are hemmed in by the tasteless concrete, glass and brick of modern shops and offices.

Fortunately, many of our finest cathedrals are now floodlit at night to illuminate the stonemason's art with even greater clarity than can be achieved in daylight. Distracting intrusions are lost in the darkness, allowing one to focus on the sheer majesty of the church itself.

Finding a good viewpoint can often be difficult amid narrow streets and tall, overhanging buildings, though this problem can surprisingly often be solved by a quick tour round a city's multi-storey car parks. These necessary evils can become ideal viewing platforms, and for no more than a minimal charge one can enjoy an unexpected perspective on a building usually only seen from ground level. Canterbury has one of the finest cathedrals in the country (see p. 44) and the local planners have sited a car park in just about the most perfect vantage point.

ST BENEDICT (480–*c.* 547) was an Italian monk who transformed monasticism from a solitary, self-searching life of denial led by hermits into a communal brotherhood following a strict daily timetable of work and prayer. Benedict developed his ideas after realizing that personal privation was a selfish and inadequate way of accomplishing God's work on Earth. He proceeded to establish a total of fourteen Italian monasteries, the first located in the mountains between Rome and Naples at Monte Cassino in 529.

Benedictinism was introduced into Britain by St Augustine's mission towards the end of the sixth century, and his monastery at Canterbury was the first Benedictine house to be founded on English soil. Once that had been successfully settled, other foundations were established in Rochester and London in the south-east, in Wessex with the mighty house of Glastonbury and further north in locations such as Winchester and Worcester. Despite the population's sporadic reluctance to reject paganism in favour of Christianity, there was a period of stability and growth throughout the country during the seventh century – until the first Viking long ships appeared over the horizon.

Danish invasion and occupation virtually obliterated English monasticism, and during this time many cathedrals replaced monks with canons. It was not until peace was fully restored during the tenth century that a renaissance occurred, led almost single-handed by Dunstan, who was appointed abbot of Glastonbury in 940.

Under Dunstan's leadership, Glastonbury became renowned as a cultural centre, attracting not only royal patronage but devoted supporters who, inspired by his leadership, returned to cathedrals such as Winchester, ejected the clergy and reinstated Benedictine monks, whose tenure would last for over five centuries.

Many of the dioceses and episcopal sees into which England is divided were first created under Saxon influence, with several remaining in place after the Conquest despite considerable reorganization of the religious landscape towards the end of the eleventh century. The Benedictine influence was very strong in Normandy and this was brought over with the new rulers. They established new monasteries, ensuring that all cathedrals were located in major towns and, perhaps most controversially, replacing English abbots with French and Norman equivalents. Many of those imported by William were highly educated men of considerable ability. They injected a sense of purpose into flagging communities and ensured that the century following the Norman Conquest became a period of great prosperity for the Benedictines.

The conduct of all those joining a monastery was governed by a set of exacting guidelines, handwritten by the founder and known as the 'Rule of St Benedict'. All Benedictine houses were strictly bound by the code and each monk was obliged formally to take the vows upon acceptance into the order. They agreed to lifelong personal poverty, chastity, total obedience to the abbot and the Rule and a commitment to remain within the order for life.

Life in all Benedictine monasteries followed a timetable divided into three distinct areas of activity, the most important being the eight fixed periods of church worship known as the 'opus Dei' – the Work of God. This centred around the Psalms, and it was expected that all 150 of them would be recited or chanted every week. Benedict had decreed that monks should sleep fully clothed to minimize delay in beginning the daily round of prayer at the dauntingly early hour of 2 a.m., although he did display a touch of compassion by instructing that the first psalm of that service should be said slowly, perhaps acknowledging that lateness was inevitable as not every brother would be skipping down the night stairs with boundless enthusiasm.

Work in the cloisters occupied a significant portion of each day, which was spent not only in private meditation but also in translating and copying religious manuscripts and other works. Many were illuminated in spectacular fashion, displaying artistic prowess of the highest degree. Artistic talent and endeavour were not the sole requirements for such a project, as a book that size would have required the skins of around two hundred and fifty calves to provide a sufficient quantity of vellum.

Manual labour was an essential component of monastic life, not simply in terms of the daily maintenance of buildings, but also food production through agriculture and the manufacture of clothing and utensils.

Unlike orders that followed later in the monastic cycle, Benedictine monasteries were not in any way linked or dependent on each other for revenue or support, their only common bond being the Rule of St Benedict.

ROOD SCREENS

Roods were representations of Christ on the Cross, usually attended by the Virgin Mary and St John the Evangelist, and were mostly supported by a screen that divided nave and chancel. As the rood was the focal point of medieval churches, the screens below were decorated with the utmost skill by masons, carpenters and artists. Those made from stone were elaborately carved with statues of saints and other religious figures, and where wood was employed, similar subjects were painted and gilded in colourful fashion.

All those individual expressions of devotion were swept away when the Reformation wrought havoc in the nation's churches during the mid-sixteenth century. Chantries were abolished, statues defaced, wall paintings obliterated with whitewash and the veneration of saints abolished. Many rood screens were simply torn down or had their original paintings covered over with passages from Cranmer's new English Prayer Book or other appropriate texts of the Protestant religion, which was forced on the population by the Act of Uniformity for public worship. Although he caused so much disruption within the Church, Henry VIII had at least attempted to pursue a placatory middle course, a tactic abandoned with some ferocity by those who manipulated his infant successor, Edward VI.

This touching fragment from the rood screen at Binham Priory (see p. 62) seems to encapsulate perfectly the anguish of those troubled times.

ST AUGUSTINE'S ABBEY, CANTERBURY, KENT

The site traditionally attributed to St Augustine's landing on English soil is marked by a nineteenth-century replica of a Celtic cross, now located a short distance inland from Cliffsend in Pegwell Bay where Augustine finally waded ashore with his group of monks in 597. Long-distance travel is very much taken for granted nowadays so one can scarcely imagine the hardships that would have been endured by the missionaries as they travelled across Europe from Rome on the instructions of Pope Gregory. The band must have encountered early difficulties, as records show that Augustine turned back after two months on the road, pleading with the Pope to be relieved of his task, but to no avail – a pontifical finger pointed firmly northwards and so back over the Alps he and his supporters went.

St Augustine's Abbey is frequently overlooked by visitors pursuing an itinerary centred around the cathedral (see p. 44) and Canterbury's narrow medieval streets, but to do so would be to miss an opportunity to explore the place from which the flame of Christianity was rekindled in England during the sixth century.

The land for this foundation was presented to Augustine by his first convert, King Ethelbert of Kent, in order to build a monastery for the monks who had accompanied him on his mission and to establish a burial site for kings and archbishops, thereby maintaining the Roman tradition of

interment outside the city walls. A major post-Conquest rebuilding programme obliterated much of the Saxon work, but traces do remain, notably in the St Pancras chapel located a short distance from the main body of the site and consequently not demolished to make way for the Norman abbey. Archaeological research has also uncovered substantial portions of the Saxon foundation, which, along with the Norman crypt, forms the centrepiece of the site.

The northern wall of the Norman nave is the tallest surviving fragment, its height increased by courses of red brick, added after the Dissolution when parts of the medieval monastery were converted into a royal residence by Henry VIII, as Canterbury at that time was a convenient staging post between London and the Channel ports.

An indication of just how huge the complex must have been can be gleaned from the fact that stone from the site was still being sold off twenty years after the Dissolution.

The abbey's history is not that easy to trace by visual inspection alone, a problem admirably solved by English Heritage, which has established a stunning entrance museum and provided taped audio guides highlighting each stage of development through the ages.

RECULVER ABBEY, HERNE BAY, KENT

Reculver Abbey was founded in 669, built on a site earlier used by the Romans for their coastal fort, Regulbium. The abandoned outpost provided not merely ample construction materials, but also, through its previous occupants, a symbolic link with the power of Rome. Well-documented histories of Saxon monasteries are rare, but at least Reculver will be remembered through the surviving fragments of a large Celtic cross now preserved in the crypt of Canterbury Cathedral. It was reputed to have been some four metres tall and embellished with elaborately detailed carving depicting the life of Christ. Following the Conquest, Reculver was adopted for parish use and was substantially enlarged during the Middle Ages when spires were added to the twelfth-century twin towers. However, as time passed, coastal erosion brought church and sea too close together for comfort, so a new parish church had to be built inland to avoid the prospect of an unscheduled and rather salty communal baptism one storm-lashed Sunday morning. After the surviving ruins were demolished in 1809, Trinity House, England's lighthouse authority, elected to rebuild the church's western façade and twin towers, which had for so long proved an invaluable navigational aid to shipping.

GLASTONBURY ABBEY, GLASTONBURY, SOMERSET

Rising above the flooded meadows of the Somerset Levels, Glastonbury is associated with many romantic myths, the fostering of which no doubt helped increase the town's status as a place of pilgrimage and consequently its wealth. According to legend, Glastonbury Tor was the mystical Isle of Avalon, King Arthur is buried in the abbey and the Holy Grail now rests beneath Chalice Spring, having been brought over from Jerusalem by Joseph of Aramathea. What cannot be disputed is that Glastonbury was a very early Christian foundation; a monastery definitely existed here in the seventh century, but it was after Dunstan became abbot in 940 that the abbey became established as one of the most powerful and influential in England. He was a great reformer of the Benedictine order and went on to become Archbishop of Canterbury. Much of the once-great abbey has been reduced to fragmented ruins, although curiously enough, the fourteenth-century abbot's kitchen is virtually intact, now standing alone and resembling an ornate salt shaker. Evidence of the abbey's status is seen in the size of the church, which was some 550 feet in length, and the impressive abbot's guesthouse, now transformed into the George and Pilgrim Hotel. The last abbot of Glastonbury, Richard Whyting, did not receive the customary pension when his abbey was dissolved, as Henry VIII decided to hang him for alleged treason.

WESTMINSTER ABBEY, LONDON

It is hard to imagine Westminster at the time of the Conquest, when it occupied an island site amid the marshes that flanked the Thames. Since William the Conqueror received the English crown here on Christmas Day 1066, coronations have always been conducted in Westminster Abbey.

An earlier Saxon monastery was completely destroyed by the Danes during the eighth century. Westminster's history as a Benedictine house dates to its foundation by St Dunstan in 959, although it was Edward the Confessor who established its status as the royal church of England following its consecration on 28 December 1065, just one week before his death.

Henry III was largely responsible for building the magnificent abbey church that stands today, work on which began in 1245, favouring the French Gothic style, which placed greater emphasis on height than the particular English interpretation that had evolved by then. Flying buttresses were used as a means of supporting the height of French cathedrals, a technique deemed visually ugly by English builders, who preferred to restrict the height and use internal methods of support.

Work on the new church advanced rapidly, and it was reopened in 1269. Although much of the nave was not completed until well over a century later, fortunately the architect was content to follow the style of his predecessor, thereby maintaining visual continuity.

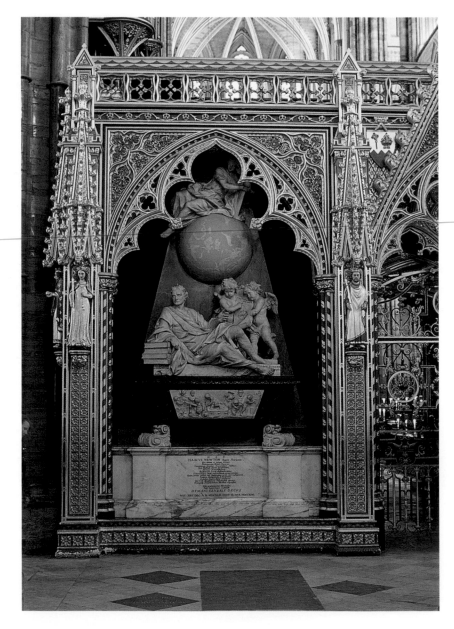

Westminster Abbey is not merely a church of unsurpassed beauty; it is also the last resting place of English monarchs – from Henry III in 1272 to George III in 1820.

Without doubt, the abbey's sublime architectural achievement is the Henry VII chapel, originally founded by that monarch early in the sixteenth century with the intention of creating a shrine to Henry VI. This plan never came to fruition and so the masterpiece of royal mason Robert Vertue was adopted by its instigator for himself and his queen, Elizabeth.

The fan-vaulted ceiling is elaborately decorated with the most complex tracery imaginable, the finest example of that art form in England. Almost every square inch of the chapel seems to be adorned with some form of intricate decoration and, although the overall effect can be almost overwhelming, it remains a quite breathtaking piece of work. The royal tomb in the chapel is the work of a Florentine contemporary of Michelangelo, sculptor Pietro Torrigiano, who was commissioned to create the most moving, gilt-bronzed effigies of Henry and Elizabeth. However, kings and queens are not the only ones celebrated in death; the abbey houses the Grave to the Unknown Soldier, a nation's tribute to those slain during the First World War. Famous names from the arts, literature and science mingle with numerous outrageously ostentatious memorials erected to members of the nobility.

WINCHESTER CATHEDRAL, WINCHESTER, HAMPSHIRE

Winchester Cathedral is the second longest in Europe after St Peter's in Rome, a fact one would readily dispute based on external assessment alone, as the building somehow fails to create an impression of great length. As soon as one enters the soaring, fourteenth-century, Perpendicular nave, however, such doubts are dispelled and the church seems to stretch to infinity beyond the choir screen, certainly appearing even longer than its actual 556 feet.

Work on the present church began in 1079 under the direction of Bishop Walkelin to replace the huge Saxon foundation of Old Minster that housed the relics of St Swithun, a ninth-century bishop whose name is forever associated with wet English summers. A shrine was eventually erected to Swithun in the new church, and became an important place of pilgrimage; for a time, only Thomas à Becket's shrine in Canterbury was more visited. Romanesque architecture from that first phase of reconstruction survives intact in both north and south transepts and also in the crypt, which is now prone to flooding in winter. Problems with Winchester's raised water table had seriously threatened the cathedral's very survival at the turn of the century when it was discovered that the original timber foundations were disintegrating and causing structural instability. The cathedral's saviour is generally acknowledged as William Walker, a

deep-sea diver who spent five years working in up to 20 feet of water, underpinning the walls by replacing rotten timbers and layers of soggy peat with countless bags of cement. Winchester was once capital of Wessex and then of all England during the reign of Alfred the Great, a status it retained until well after the Norman Conquest when it was gradually eclipsed by London. One of the most lavish royal events to have taken place in the cathedral was the post-Dissolution wedding of Mary Tudor to Philip of Spain in 1554, ironically the same person who, as King of Spain, would later be sending his Armada to interrupt Sir Francis Drake's game of bowls in Plymouth.

Several of the Saxon kings who were crowned and buried here are represented by their colourfully inscribed mortuary chests. These line the presbytery, which is dominated by the massive, fifteenth-century stone screen whose many delicately carved niches are filled with quite superb modern replicas of the original saints' statues that were desecrated and smashed during the Reformation. That Winchester's windows were once adorned by sumptuous displays of painted glass is evident from those fragments that survived the vandalism inflicted on the church by Cromwell's Parliamentarian troops during the Civil War. The confusing, coloured patchwork of the nave's west window was created from shards and segments rescued from the shattered original

and reconstituted in its current form after the Restoration of the monarchy in 1660.

Medieval glass may now be poorly represented but there are some outstanding modern examples of the genre, most notably the designs by Edward Burne-Jones in the four windows of the Epiphany chapel. The glass, made by the William Morris workshops, is remarkable for its intensity and depth of colour.

Despite being less colourful than the glass, the cathedral's collection of thirteenth-century floor tiles is no less impressive and forms the largest spread in England. Mainly centred around the retrochoir, the encaustic tiles feature a number of designs varying from simple geometric patterns to more elaborate heraldic symbols and fleurs-de-lys. A basic, red, Wessex clay tile was imprinted using a wooden stamp or similar device while still malleable, and the resulting mould was then filled with a contrasting white clay, after which the combination was glazed and fired. Although some sections have been roped off to prevent further wear and tear, substantial areas are still trodden daily by visitors, pilgrims and clergy alike, much as they have been for the past 700 years.

ROMSEY ABBEY, ROMSEY, HAMPSHIRE

Romsey Abbey represents one of the finest surviving examples of Late Norman architecture, fortuitously purchased intact by the town during the Dissolution for £100. The abbey's history goes back to Saxon times, and ever since Alfred the Great's granddaughter, Eflaeda, was installed as the first abbess, Romsey always housed a nunnery.

Around 967, the abbey was re-founded under Benedictine rule, but the nuns were forced to flee to the safety of Winchester when the abbey was attacked by Danes. When peace was once more established, the nuns returned to Romsey to begin the process of rebuilding, a stone church replacing the burnt-out shell of its predecessor.

In those pre-Conquest times, Romsey achieved a reputation as a place of learning, a safe haven where Saxon nobility could send their daughters to be educated in religion and other subjects in a sympathetic environment. However, in common with many other 'finishing schools', the students were not totally cut off from outside influences, as one of their number, Eadyth, a daughter of Margaret, Queen of Scotland, was successfully courted by Henry I.

Romsey is in the enviable position of possessing two Saxon roods, one inside the church and a larger one outside on the south transept wall. The south choir aisle ends in an apsidal Norman chapel

in which is located a small, low relief sculpture of the Crucifixion – a work of outstanding clarity for its age. The white stone figures are thrown into sharp relief by a gold painted background, simulating the original gilding. Not surprisingly, the precious stones that once adorned the participants' eyes have been prised from their sockets, but no jewels are really needed to enrich this work, which portrays the moment when Christ is offered a vinegar-soaked sponge to assuage his thirst.

The exterior rood is next to the extravagantly decorated abbess's door, which originally led out into the cloisters. The carving is protected from further weather damage by a wooden canopy, and although erosion has robbed the statue of finer detail, the intent of the artist is plain to see. Extending from heavenly clouds, the hand of God points down towards his son who, although still on the cross, has his arms and hands in an attitude of welcome. By the use of such devices, both roods transmit the same message, namely that death is only the beginning. Inlaid into the floor of the south transept is a simple memorial to Earl Mountbatten of Burma, who lived nearby on the country estate of Broadlands, which was passed by inheritance to Lady Mountbatten from the Palmerston family, one of whose members was a formidable prime minister during Queen Victoria's reign. Directly above the Mountbatten stone is an altogether fancier affair,

celebrating John and Grisel St Barbe, owners of Broadlands before the Palmerston dynasty. Mr and Mrs Barbe are carved and painted in what appears almost photographic detail, accompanied at the foot of the memorial by their four children. The stonework in both nave and chancel is of the highest quality, especially in the latter where tier upon tier of rounded arches disappear into the roof's dark recesses. Romsey's triforium is unusual for its smaller, twin arches that occupy each bay, decorated with varying degrees of dog-tooth carving.

In direct contrast to the powerful Norman interior, the St Lawrence chapel displays an early sixteenth-century painted reredos that is lucky to have survived the Reformation. The upper portion is devoted to full length figures of various saints, while the bottom half shows the risen Christ in fairly jaunty mood, flanked by censer-wielding angels and a couple of less than enthusiastic soldiers in medieval armour. Also featured is the figure of a nun waving a slender banner covered in text conveying the message of the painting; probably a portrait of the abbess who commissioned the work.

ST ALBANS CATHEDRAL ABBEY, ST ALBANS, HERTFORDSHIRE

Alban was England's first Christian martyr, executed for his beliefs by the Romans early in the fourth century. None of the building from earlier monasteries established on Alban's tomb has survived, and the mighty abbey church around which the city of St Albans grew was started by the first Norman abbot, Paul of Caen. As there were no local sources of stone, the builders utilized brick from the adjacent ruined Roman city of Verulamium. St Albans took highest rank among medieval abbeys, favoured by a decree from Pope Adrian IV in 1154 declaring that its abbot should be the senior mitred abbot in Parliament. It may be coincidental, but that particular pontiff was the only pope to come from England, Nicholas Breakspear, born not far from St Albans. A case of nepotism, perhaps? The church has a long nave of twelve bays, some pillars of which are decorated with recently restored medieval wall paintings, helping to alleviate Norman austerity. Medieval designs have been repainted on to the wooden chancel ceiling, providing a perfect visual foil for the exquisite stone screen beneath. Nineteenth-century restoration, although vital in preserving much of the abbey's fabric, was less than sympathetic to the abbey's origins, as a glance at the west front proves. Although work was generously financed by Lord Grimthorpe, a Victorian architect and lawyer, unfortunately he insisted on his own restoration plans.

WORCESTER CATHEDRAL PRIORY, WORCESTER, WORCESTERSHIRE

No scene could be more quintessentially English than a game of cricket played in the shadow of a medieval cathedral, a tableau to be seen regularly in Worcester during the summer and captured in photographs that adorn countless calendars, chocolate boxes and postcards. However attractive that view may be, it fails to show the cathedral in its incomparable setting on the River Severn. It is especially atmospheric after dusk when illuminated and the west front and fourteenth-century tower cast golden reflections on to the waters below.

The Diocese of Worcester was created in 680 with Bosel as its first bishop, although his seventh-century cathedral, dedicated to St Peter, would have been a relatively primitive structure. It was not until the tenth century that Oswald, encouraged by enthusiastic support from King Edgar, established a Benedictine house re-dedicated to St Mary. Unfortunately, that was burnt to the ground by a Danish raiding party, and only in 1062, when Prior Wulfstan was appointed bishop, did Worcester's regeneration begin. Wulfstan was one of the leading lights of Saxon Christianity and was so highly regarded for his knowledge, devoutness and preaching that he was the only Anglo-Saxon bishop not to be replaced by a Norman appointee after the Conquest.

In 1084 work began on a new cathedral, the very heart of which survives today in the Romanesque crypt, the largest in England and built by Wulfstan to house St Oswald's shrine. Some church crypts survive as mere empty shells, their dark fusty interiors reflecting the passage of time, but Worcester has restored its own to a place of worship. Services are held there on a regular basis, although modern seating and excessively harsh lighting detract from the atmosphere created by the stumpy Norman pillars and rounded arches.

In addition to the crypt, Norman architecture is most noticeably featured in the circular chapter house, the lower stage of which is covered in elegant blank arcading. Of even greater appeal are the slender, semicircular vaulting ribs emanating from one single central column in a burst of contrasting colour, as though cascading from an exploding firework.

The church did not enjoy the best of fortune during the twelfth century, when its fabric was badly damaged by fire, civil war during Stephen's reign and a collapsing crossing tower in 1175. Restoration and rebuilding during the following century were greatly assisted by the influx of pilgrims, whose donations ensured the stonemasons were kept fully occupied. Following Wulfstan's canonization in 1203, King John elected to be buried in the cathedral on his death in 1216, thus increasing Worcester's financially lucrative collection to two saints and a monarch.

King John's tomb lies in the chancel in front of the high altar, his coffin lid of

Purbeck marble bearing the earliest
surviving effigy of an English ruler.
This most beautiful part of the church
is thirteenth-century Early English,
representing the most productive and
creative period of the English style of
Gothic architecture. The dark marble
used for John's tomb was also utilized
to great effect as a contrasting medium,
emphasizing the height and slender
form of narrow, elegant arches
and windows.

Most of the nave's construction was
carried out during the fourteenth
century, although the presence of both
Decorated and Perpendicular styles
suggests there might have been a quite
substantial lull midway through that
phase. The delay could possibly be
attributed to the Black Death, which
decimated the population of Western
Europe, or perhaps even to a lack of
funds, as pilgrims could have taken
their business down the road to Edward
II's shrine at Gloucester (see p. 49).
Every August, the nave is emptied of all
pews and seating to enable cleaning and
other essential maintenance to be
carried out, providing a perfect
opportunity to experience the
cathedral's interior as it would have
appeared centuries ago – a vast space of
light and shade, extending for over 400
feet from the west window towards the
altar. There is, however, one jarring note
in the composition – the Victorian
black and white tiled floor, which seems
so inappropriate in the midst of stone,
medieval monuments and the muted
colours of stained glass. It is one of

those features that will have supporters
and detractors in equal numbers, but
my own opinion is that such a floor
covering would be more appropriate to
an Italian restaurant than the entire nave
of a gracious church.

Design considerations aside, the
nineteenth-century restoration was very
necessary and, although much of the
work has introduced a blandness to
parts of the cathedral's exterior, had it
not been carried out, the building's very
survival might have been in jeopardy.
In addition to the royal tomb of King
John, Worcester also houses the
sumptuous chantry tomb of Prince
Arthur, Henry VIII's elder brother, and
with it, one of the great conundrums of
religious history. If Arthur had acceded
to the throne instead of dying
prematurely aged only fifteen, would the
Dissolution have taken place, or was it
an inevitable process, regardless of
which monarch occupied the throne? In
order to preserve the vital Spanish
alliance, Henry married Arthur's widow,
Catherine of Aragon, and again one
could contemplate the likely course of
history had he not divorced her for
failing to produce a male heir.
Arthur's chantry is richly adorned with
statuary both inside and out, and the
single stone step leading into the
enclosed space has been smoothed into
a deep concave outline by centuries of
pilgrims' feet.

ELY CATHEDRAL PRIORY, ELY, CAMBRIDGESHIRE

As might be deduced from its spelling, Ely is translated as 'Isle of Eels', a reference to the potentially tedious staple diet of the Saxons who inhabited this elevated undulation amid the watery landscape. That such a mighty cathedral and monastery were built here long before the Fens were drained is remarkable, a lasting testimony to those who regarded natural hazards as challenges to be overcome for the glory of God. The religious house on Ely has existed in various guises since 673 when it was founded by Etheldreda, initially for both nuns and monks. Later, in the tenth century, it was converted to a Benedictine abbey at the behest of King Edgar, and it was from here that the folk hero Hereward the Wake established his guerrilla base during an ultimately fruitless post-Conquest campaign against William I in 1070. Ely Cathedral still dominates the flat countryside, a landmark visible for miles in any direction, and its distinctive silhouette creates a particularly atmospheric image when viewed against the lurid colours generated by a pre-dawn winter sky. William appointed Simeon, an elderly Norman abbot, to take charge of Ely, and a rebuilding programme was instigated in 1083, although the nave was not completed until 1189. Its walls are 86 feet high, and to counter that extra height they were never burdened with a vaulted roof, a lighter timber construction being used instead.

During much-needed Victorian restoration work, the nave roof was boarded over and what at first glance might be taken for a sumptuous medieval painted ceiling dates only from the mid-nineteenth century, though it is no less glorious for being so recently completed. At the crossing end of the nave, one approaches Ely's architectural jewel, the octagon and lantern tower, arguably one of the greatest feats of medieval engineering and design anywhere. In 1322 the central tower collapsed 'with a roar like thunder, of shock and so great a tumult', leaving a large, gaping hole in the roof. Cathedral sacrist Alan of Walsingham, who was in charge of building projects during that period, conceived the revolutionary feature that even today many architects would be reluctant to risk bringing to fruition. Extending up from the lower octagon, an inner lantern was created using eight long upright sections of oak (virtually the whole tree trunk), supported by a complex geometric network of wooden struts, the weight being transferred downwards and out towards the octagon walls and pillars. Standing directly beneath the glazed and colourfully painted lantern, it is difficult for the layman to grasp fully how over 400 tons of timber and lead can seem so effortlessly suspended.

MALMESBURY ABBEY, MALMESBURY, WILTSHIRE

Malmesbury claims to be one of the oldest boroughs in England, having strong links with Alfred the Great's grandson, the Saxon monarch King Athelstan, who ruled from 925 to 940. Athelstan was a patron of the abbey originally founded by St Aldhelm in the seventh century – a fifteenth-century table tomb with reclining effigy commemorating the monarch can be found inside the church. A parish church has been fashioned from six bays of the nave, which formed part of the abbey church, work on which began in 1143. The massive Norman pillars of the interior are starkly contrasted with the delicately carved south porch; it is considered to be one of the finest examples of Romanesque carving in the country, and the receding layered arches depict saints and biblical scenes. During the fourteenth century, a spire was added to the crossing tower, its height reputed to have exceeded that of Salisbury Cathedral, which at 404 feet is England's tallest. As if to make a statement, Malmesbury's tower and spire collapsed just prior to the Dissolution. Defying gravity was also foremost in the mind of one of the abbey's eleventh-century monks, Elmer, who equipped himself with home-made wings and attempted to fly from the tower, breaking both legs in the process and being crippled for life. His 'achievement' is now celebrated by a modern stained-glass window inside the church.

CROYLAND ABBEY, CROWLAND, LINCOLNSHIRE

Croyland Abbey is now the parish church of Crowland, the north aisle having been retained at the Dissolution. The magnificently sculpted thirteenth-century west front of the nave has also survived, its huge empty window starkly silhouetted against the empty Fenland sky. When St Guthlac chose Crowland for his hermitage at the end of the seventh century, the Fens consisted of small, inhospitable islands set amid great tracts of treacherous bog. Despite his isolation, Guthlac attracted many devotees, one of whom was Ethelbald, a future king of Mercia. He vowed to Guthlac that if he should attain the throne, he would build a monastery on that site as a token of thanksgiving. Ethelbald kept his word and two years after Guthlac's death in 716, the foundations for the first monastery were laid. During the ninth century, Croyland fell prey to Danish invaders who not only wrecked the buildings but slaughtered the abbot and several monks who were celebrating Mass at the time. Subsequent replacements were also victims of a series of disasters, including an earthquake in 1118. Croyland has always been renowned for its bells, as it produced the first tuned peal in the country, cast by Abbots Turketyl and Egelric towards the end of the tenth century. The great bell was christened Guthlac, while its six companions rejoiced in the names of Bartholomew and Beccelm, Turketyl and Tatwin, and Pega and Bega.

CANTERBURY CATHEDRAL PRIORY, CANTERBURY, KENT

Canterbury Cathedral's 250-foot central tower, 'Bell Harry', dominates the medieval core of the city originally named Durovernum by the Romans, who established a fortified centre here around AD 43, on the site of an even earlier settlement. Canterbury's name originates from the Saxon phrase 'Cant-wara-byrig', which translates as 'the borough of the men of Kent'. The city was the home of King Ethelbert, St Augustine's initial convert on his evangelical crusade to bring Christianity back to England after the Dark Ages. His first cathedral was built here, making Canterbury the cradle of English Christianity and, subsequently, Mother Church of the Anglican religion throughout the world.

Strange quirks of fate have often contributed to the shaping of history and one should perhaps be grateful that Ethelbert was based in Canterbury rather than another Kentish town. Addressing the Primate of all England as 'Archbishop of Ramsgate' somehow lacks the dignified resonance of 'Canterbury'.

Consider also the actions of Henry II's knights against Thomas à Becket on 29 December 1170, who, in response to their monarch's exasperated but probably rhetorical question, 'Will no one rid me of this turbulent priest?', sought to curry favour by heading forthwith for Canterbury and murdering the unfortunate archbishop in his own cathedral.

Becket's martyrdom and subsequent enshrinement led to Canterbury becoming the greatest place of pilgrimage in the country. This generated vast additional revenue, which proved invaluable when it became necessary to rebuild the cathedral after a disastrous fire in 1174, just four years after Becket's death. It was from that date that the cathedral that exists today began to evolve. Was the fire divine retribution? If not and had Becket died naturally, would reconstruction on such a lavish scale have been possible without pilgrim-generated income? Of course, without pilgrims, Chaucer could not have written his medieval masterpiece *The Canterbury Tales* (no doubt to the relief of countless students of English literature).

The fire of 1174 was not the first calamity to befall the cathedral since its re-founding as a Benedictine house in 997. The Danes had wreaked havoc at the start of the eleventh century, followed in 1067, shortly after the Conquest, by a fire that all but gutted the building. William I installed Lanfranc of Bec as archbishop to restore the cathedral and, although his work was largely obliterated by the later fire, those charged with renovating Lanfranc's building largely adhered to his original ground plan.

Reconstruction of Canterbury's interior was undertaken during two separate phases of development, separated by 200 years. William of Sens was primarily responsible for the choir and eastern end of the church, although his

intended designs for the Trinity chapel and corona were probably completed by another builder, as William had to retire from the project through serious injury following a fall from scaffolding inside the church.

The nave was the work of Henry Yevele, a builder of outstanding talent who served two successive monarchs, Edward III and Richard II. For such a huge enclosed arena, the nave seems particularly well lit, an effect contrived by introducing higher arcades and ensuring that large windows were located directly opposite their openings, thus maximizing available daylight. The overall length of the church is in excess of 500 feet and one can scarcely imagine the awe felt by pilgrims as they progressed eastwards, with cleverly placed flights of steps through nave and choir creating a sensation of triumphant ascension towards the high altar and Becket's golden, jewel-encrusted shrine in the Trinity chapel beyond.

An impression of Canterbury's true atmosphere can be gained when the cathedral reverts to being a place of worship, instead of a tourist attraction. Choral evensong on a winter's afternoon can recreate some of that aura of mystery, when all lights are extinguished save for those in the choir and the chorister's spine-tingling anthems reverberate out into the nave's cavernous void.

Henry VIII may have destroyed Thomas à Becket's shrine, but there are many other details and treasures to absorb

and delight one. Canterbury's surviving medieval stained glass is some of the finest and most colourful in England, depicting not just traditional biblical scenes and characters, but also those associated with aspects of pilgrimage. Of the many tombs and effigies, one of the most impressive is that of Edward the Black Prince, son of Edward III and renowned for his brilliant victory over the French at Poitiers in 1356.

One sight in the cathedral that should not be missed is the view looking up inside John Wastell's magnificent tower, built around 1500, its ceiling adorned with the most delicate fan vaulting. Staring up into that narrow space, so far from the ground, one wonders how such a task was accomplished.

As one might expect of a monastery of Canterbury's stature, the monastic range was extensive, including a dormitory to accommodate up to a hundred and fifty, a large infirmary and a latrine block delightfully referred to on a twelfth-century plan as the 'necessarium'. The lierne-vaulted cloisters are beautifully preserved and still offer a haven for quiet reflection, much as they did six centuries ago when they were rebuilt by Prior Chillenden.

BURY ST EDMUNDS ABBEY, BURY ST EDMUNDS, SUFFOLK

How sad it is to see most of one of England's greatest medieval abbeys reduced to little more than a collection of sculptured rubble in a public park. This is in stark contrast to the evidence of former grandeur that survives in the fourteenth-century Great Gate, which once gave access to the great court and abbot's palace.

Originally known as Beodricsworth, Bury acquired its present name from the East Anglian king, subsequently canonized, whose body was enshrined here some thirty years after being martyred by the Danes in 870. The Benedictine house was first granted a charter by King Canute in 1021, and once established it grew rapidly more powerful, benefiting particularly from the wealth generated by Suffolk's flourishing and extremely lucrative wool trade. It was on the abbey's high altar that the barons who forced King John into signing the Magna Carta at Runnymede in 1215 had sworn their pact to exact concessions of greater civil liberties from the king a year earlier. As the abbey's prosperity increased, the town's inhabitants grew more resentful of the demands made upon them by the monastic community. Unrest escalated into violence at least twice during the fourteenth century, most notably during the Peasants' Revolt of 1381, which resulted in looting, serious damage to monastery buildings and several murders.

GLOUCESTER CATHEDRAL PRIORY, GLOUCESTER, GLOUCESTERSHIRE

Its status as the lowest crossing point on the River Severn made Gloucester commercially and militarily strategic, a fact recognized by William I, who revitalized the ailing Benedictine monastery that existed at the time of the Conquest. Gloucester was one of the monastic churches retained as cathedrals by Henry VIII, possibly because of its many royal associations. Henry III was crowned here in 1216 aged only nine, and over a century later Edward II was interred here after his gruesome murder in nearby Berkeley Castle. It seems ironic that a monarch reviled during his reign as an effeminate wimp should have been so venerated after his death that his elegant alabaster tomb became a place of pilgrimage, generating wealth that enabled a remodelling of the chancel in the Perpendicular style. This purely English variation was pioneered in Gloucester and became the last great phase of Gothic architecture. Of the claustral buildings, only the chapter house is in regular use, fulfilling the same function it has for centuries, but it is the cloisters that are Gloucester's ancient treasure. Recesses that used to house wooden desks for reading or writing occupy one section, while another retains the original wash place used by the monks before dining in the adjacent frater, all adorned with the most exquisite fan vaulting, the first time such a technique was used for claustral decoration.

BATTLE ABBEY, BATTLE, EAST SUSSEX

Battle Abbey's fortified gatehouse, which dominates one end of the village High Street, was erected during the fourteenth century in response to persistent French cross-Channel raids. It is perhaps ironic that the abbey owes its very existence to an earlier Norman invader whose own intended plunder was no less a prize than the English throne. The abbey was founded by William the Conqueror, both as an act of thanksgiving for victory and a penance for those slain in the bloody conflict. The date 1066 seems to be one of the few dates in English history that has not faded from popular recall. Perhaps the Battle of Hastings has simply stuck in the minds of generations of ghoulish schoolchildren because of the grisly manner in which King Harold of England allegedly met his end – an unfortunate glance skyward coinciding with the rapid downward trajectory of a Norman arrow. William's insistence that the abbey should occupy the exact battle site and that the church's high altar should be placed directly over the spot where Harold died caused almost insurmountable problems. The elevated, sloping site may have favoured military tactics, but in terms of construction, water supply, drainage and other factors, it would have been readily

dismissed by the monks had they been given carte blanche. Although sections of the abbey are well preserved, the church was totally destroyed at the Dissolution. Excavations have enabled archaeologists to produce a fairly accurate ground plan, but the total absence of the abbey's focal point is a cause of great sadness. Many monasteries were allowed to retain part of the church for parish worship, but as a separate church already existed outside the precinct walls, no case could be made for a stay of execution. Of the buildings that have survived, the novices' room and monks' common room located below the now-roofless dormitory in the east range are both wonderfully atmospheric chambers, the former having a particularly lofty vaulted ceiling supported on marble columns. On the opposite side of the cloister, the west range housed the abbot's lodgings and great hall, used for entertaining distinguished guests, buildings that were easily converted into a mansion after the Dissolution by Sir Robert Browne, friend of Henry VIII and Master of the Horse. The hall is open to visitors but only during midsummer, as the buildings now form part of Battle Abbey School. A rather dark vaulted parlour adjacent to the hall probably serves as the pupils' dining room, as evidenced by the neat rows of tables and that unforgettable, lingering aroma of school dinners.

ROCHESTER CATHEDRAL PRIORY, ROCHESTER, KENT

Occupying a strategic crossing point on the lower reaches of the River Medway, Rochester has been settled since pre-Roman times and, along with neighbouring Chatham, has long been associated with British naval history. Despite being surrounded by dockyards and modern industrial sites, Rochester has managed to keep its quaint city centre intact. Charles Dickens had close ties with the area, and there are many references to Rochester in his novels. One gets the impression that Rochester has often been held in lower esteem than other cathedrals, but its place in the 'second division' is hardly warranted. After Augustine's successful mission to Canterbury, Rochester was the next diocese to be created, making it the second oldest in England, with Justus, its first bishop, sent by Pope Gregory in 601 to assist Augustine's crusade. Of that early church, dedicated to St Andrew, nothing now remains, but archaeological research has led to the discovery of its foundations beneath the present nave.

Evidence that Church and State were once irrevocably linked is provided by the close proximity of the castle and the cathedral. Both buildings were initially the work of Gundulf, the second of William the Conqueror's newly appointed bishops, the first having been Lanfranc at Canterbury. Of the castle, only the later keep survives, but in the cathedral, Gundulf's work can still be appreciated in the crypt.

Gundulf's first church was substantially added to during a twelfth-century building programme, and Norman architecture from that phase survives in the nave, cloisters and chapter house. The enlarged cathedral was consecrated in the presence of Henry I in 1130. Two disastrous fires affected the building in the following decades, but fortunately the stonework in the nave withstood the flames and only the wooden roof perished.

The eastern part of the church was rebuilt towards the end of the twelfth century, funded by unexpected posthumous contributions from William of Perth, a benevolent baker who was murdered prior to embarking on a pilgrimage to the Holy Land. Having been laid to rest in the church, miracles were attributed to his tomb and, instead of making a pilgrimage, he became the object of one. Pilgrims were the equivalent of medieval tourists whose spending power was often vital to church and local economies, and Rochester frequently lost out to neighbouring Canterbury (see p. 44) in that respect.

Two outstanding examples of the stonemason's art are represented by the tympanum over the exterior west door, and the chapter house doorway, which was produced during the Decorated period of the mid-fourteenth century. It exhibits the most exquisite touch from the artist, and one would have to visit many churches to find a more rewarding piece of work.

WHITBY ABBEY, WHITBY, NORTH YORKSHIRE

Whitby's distinctive outline makes it not only one of the most recognizable monastic sites in England but also certainly one of the most photographed, although its popularity may have far more to do with vampires than architectural merit.

Perched high up on cliffs overlooking the Yorkshire fishing port, its gaunt silhouette can certainly appear sinister when seen against a darkening twilight sky, but how differently would it be perceived if Bram Stoker had selected another location for Dracula's landfall? The first religious foundation to occupy this site was a monastery for both nuns and monks, established by St Hilda in 657. It was later chosen as the venue for the famous synod of 664, which sought to reconcile differences between the Celtic and Roman forms of religion. That first monastery fell prey to Danish invaders and was destroyed in 867, and the site was not built on again until after the Conquest. What exists today represents but a small part of the original thirteenth-century abbey church, and engravings made during the eighteenth and early nineteenth centuries reveal how impressive it must have been in. Those same illustrations also showed piles of fallen masonry, substantially increased in later portrayals. Centuries of neglect combined with an exposed location had gradually reduced Yorkshire's third richest Benedictine house to piles of rubble, a decline now happily arrested.

ST MARY'S ABBEY, LASTINGHAM, NORTH YORKSHIRE

There are no visible monastic remains in the peaceful North Yorkshire Moors village of Lastingham, but preserved beneath the parish church of St Mary is the Norman crypt built by Abbot Stephen as a shrine to St Cedd, founder of an earlier seventh-century Saxon monastery on this site, whose remains lie buried beside the altar. Permission had been granted by William I in 1078 for a Benedictine abbey to be built as a replacement for Cedd's earlier foundation, destroyed by the Danes around 866. Having completed work on the crypt, Abbot Stephen decided to move his community away from the potentially dangerous isolation of the moors, to the greater safety and comfort of York, re-establishing a similarly dedicated abbey in the shadow of the minster. Lastingham is unique among surviving Saxon and Norman crypts in that it is a complete church in miniature, with a nave, aisles and apsidal chancel. The nave's vaulted roof is supported by short, thick pillars topped with large, decorated capitals, some of which are unembellished while others are more elaborately decorated with ram's horn swirls. Displayed along the aisle walls are carved stones from the earlier Saxon foundation. Despite its diminutive size, the crypt exudes an atmosphere of power — not merely through its solid dimensions, but by the faith and love that brought it into being.

DURHAM CATHEDRAL PRIORY, DURHAM, COUNTY DURHAM

All the superlatives so freely used about Durham Cathedral are entirely justified. Diverse opinions will always be offered regarding the relative architectural and aesthetic merits of buildings, but few would disagree that, both inside and out, Durham is truly awesome, arguably the finest surviving Romanesque church in Europe. Durham owes its existence to St Cuthbert, the great saint of northern Christianity, as its site was eventually chosen to house a permanent shrine for his remains. Having fled from Lindisfarne (see p. 58), the monks carried his still untainted body around the north-east for many years until settling on the rugged, pear-shaped sandstone outcrop, around much of which the River Wear forms a defensive moat. A humble Saxon church, dedicated in 998, was demolished to make way for the present cathedral, on which work started in 1093. When one considers the size and scale of the building, it is almost inconceivable that, excluding the towers, the church was completed in just forty years, with only the Galilee and Nine Altars chapels added later. Durham's nave is remarkable for the sheer power of its massive pillars, 27 feet high and 7 feet in diameter, alternating between plain clustered columns, deeply incised chevrons and diamonds, linked by traditional Norman dog-toothed arches. The roof featured a high rib vault, a technique that was generally used much later during the Gothic

period, making Durham a landmark in architectural design. Cuthbert now lies beneath a simple stone slab behind the high altar, his once richly adorned shrine having been plundered and desecrated at the Dissolution. At the opposite end of the church, amid the Galilee's slender columns, the Venerable Bede rests in equal simplicity, his tomb topped with a heavy piece of black marble whose surface has been smoothed and indented by countless hands over the centuries. The stalls that now fill the choir are sadly not the originals – they were burnt for firewood by the 4,000 Scottish prisoners of war incarcerated in the cathedral by Cromwell after the Battle of Dunbar in 1650. That the whole building is a shrine to one person probably accounts for the noticeable absence of ostentatious tombs and memorials normally such a feature of medieval cathedrals. This lack gives added poignancy to the memorial dedicated to the generations of Durham miners who died underground in pursuit of coal to fuel the fires of home and industry. Outside the cathedral, the cloisters are wide and solid, their exterior stonework blackened by the encrusted grime of an industrial heritage. Claustral buildings have been creatively adapted for modern use: there is now a library in the monks' dormitory; the great kitchen acts as a bookshop; and the cellar has been transformed into a most elegant café, complete with thirteenth-century pillars and vaulting.

LINDISFARNE PRIORY, LINDISFARNE (HOLY ISLAND), NORTHUMBERLAND

Few places evoke the spirit of early Christianity so much as Lindisfarne, a feeling enhanced by its separation from the Northumberland coast by a tidal causeway. As the mainland is left behind, one somehow becomes enveloped in the timeless atmosphere of Lindisfarne, an intangible, inexplicable feeling that leaves few visitors unmoved, regardless of their religious beliefs.

St Aidan, eventually drawn to Lindisfarne by its peace and isolation, founded the first community here in 635 at the invitation of King Oswald of Northumbria. That first monastery would have borne no resemblance to the surviving medieval ruins, as Aidan probably followed the Irish tradition of simple huts grouped round a basic thatched timber church.

The solid Norman priory church that occupies the site today is famous for its 'rainbow arch', that one miraculously surviving vault rib from the crossing, and it is quite extraordinary how one small fragment of stone can be so symbolic, signifying for many the enduring strength of Christianity against all odds.

Lindisfarne's history is irrevocably linked to St Cuthbert, who spent much of his devout life as a hermit on the Farne Islands, several miles further offshore, returning only to spend a short period as bishop in 685 before his death just two years later. His will

stipulated that if the monks ever left the island, then his remains should accompany them.

Having been buried beneath the church for over a decade, Cuthbert's body was disinterred for enshrinement in 698, but to the monks' amazement, his corpse was in perfect condition, exhibiting no signs of decay whatsoever. So it was reverently installed in a new wooden coffin that remained unburied by the altar.

This miraculous event was probably the inspiration behind one of Celtic Christianity's greatest treasures, the Lindisfarne Gospels. Created by Bishop Eadfrith, the work consists of 258 pages, beautifully inscribed and decorated throughout with an introduction to each Gospel featuring intricate lettering, illustration and colour of indescribable intensity.

In 793 Scandinavian raiders landed on Lindisfarne, the first such attack on the English coast and heralding an era of destruction and terror. Such harassment eventually made Lindisfarne untenable, and the monks were forced to abandon their monastery, taking Cuthbert, other relics and even their dismantled church on an odyssey that was to last for over a hundred and fifty years until they eventually settled in Durham (see p. 56). Defensive walls and towers pierced with arrow slits were a necessary part of the later Benedictine house, as Lindisfarne was close to Scotland and thereby susceptible to attack by raiding parties heading south during the cross-border conflicts of the Middle Ages.

TYNEMOUTH PRIORY, TYNEMOUTH, TYNE AND WEAR

Tynemouth Castle stands guard over the River Tyne's mouth, and the Benedictine priory is encapsulated within the safety of the gatehouse, ditch and curtain walls that encircle the rock outcrop. Such a strategic location, especially one so close to Scotland, ensured that the fortifications were constantly upgraded by successive English kings and abbots. Perhaps the most dramatic feature of the ruins is the chancel of the priory church, whose presbytery wall survives to almost full height, pierced by long narrow lancets instead of the traditional east window. Perhaps such an exposed headland position directly facing the prevailing, harsh North Sea weather precluded the use of a single large glazed area. The priory was founded as a dependency of St Albans (see p. 35) by Robert de Mowbray, Earl of Northumberland, in 1085, much to the chagrin of Durham (see p. 56), which rather thought the site was its own to administer. An earlier church and monastery certainly existed here in the seventh century and was the burial place of a local ruler, King Oswin, who was later canonized and whose tomb became a place of pilgrimage after miracles were allegedly performed there. All traces of other buildings have been obliterated, leaving the church to stand alone amid a collection of eighteenth- and nineteenth-century gravestones. The inscriptions on many are now eroded into weird patterns resembling an obscure Arabic script.

BATH ABBEY, BATH, NORTH-EAST SOMERSET

Affectionately referred to as the 'Lantern of the West' because of the light that floods into both nave and chancel through large, clear glass windows, Bath Abbey is a delightful example of Perpendicular architecture. On bright, windy days when clouds and sun alternate rapidly, light and shadow play across the exquisite fan-vaulted ceiling, creating an effect resembling delicate sea coral, with surfaces gently rippled by unseen currents. This site has been used by a succession of religious foundations since it was first occupied by Celtic nuns in 676; one of the highlights of its early history was in 963 when Edgar was crowned king of all England by St Dunstan and St Edgar. At the end of the eleventh century, Bath was designated a cathedral, but even that elevation could not prevent the church's gradual decline, and it had become almost a ruin by 1476. Construction of a new church was begun by Bishop Oliver King in 1499 as a result of a vivid dream he had in which angels clambered up and down ladders into heaven and a loud voice exhorted, 'A king to restore the church.' With his potentially ambiguous surname, the bishop could not have known whether the demand was made of him personally or of the reigning monarch, but he undertook the task anyway. His vision is recreated in unique stone sculptures on the abbey's glorious west front.

BINHAM PRIORY, NR BLAKENEY, NORFOLK

East Anglia's lack of dramatic, rolling countryside is more than compensated for by other unique landscape features, distinctive building styles and important pilgrimage sites. Indeed, Binham Priory is sandwiched midway between two such diverse locations. To the north, Blakeney's lonely creeks and coastal salt marshes contrast sharply with the organized chaos often prevailing around the Anglican and Roman Catholic shrines at Walsingham, Binham's southerly neighbour. The network of narrow lanes in Walsingham was not designed to accommodate such volumes of coach traffic, and this frequently leads to driver confrontations punctuated by most un-Christian phrases. The priory was founded as a dependency of St Albans (see p. 35) in 1091 by a nephew of William the Conqueror, Peter de Valoines. As the priory church also served the parish, much of the nave was retained at the Dissolution for continued worship. Seven of the nave's original nine bays form the present church, creating an atmosphere of stark simplicity, accentuated by the blanked-off east end, rounded Norman arches and minimal furnishings.

Details that do catch the eye are several ornately carved, sixteenth-century 'poppy-head' bench end decorations and surviving fragments of the original rood screen. At the time of the Reformation, the 'forbidden' images of saints were virtually obliterated by heavy Gothic lettering, reproducing selected Bible texts. Fortunately, time has faded the black script, allowing some of the paintings' original radiance to be seen more clearly. An access path leads through gravestones towards the church's west front, Prior Richard de Parco's fine example of Early English architecture dominated by its huge west window, now sadly filled in with red brick instead of its original elegant bar tracery. This example of that particular development in window design may well have been its earliest use in England, as the same style that is prominently featured in Westminster Abbey (see p. 26) was not installed until some time after 1245, de Parco having died with his work completed one year earlier. The priory was constructed using a combination of local flint and Barnack limestone, a material quarried in Northamptonshire that was especially favoured by the region's medieval church builders for its colour, texture and durability. The stone was transported from its source by river and sea, an arduous task but one entirely justified by the enduring quality of intricate carved detail featured on the arches and capitals either side of the main doorway. Of the monastic buildings, few have survived to any great height, but they are clearly discernible, the crossing piers of the church being the most impressive remains. Defiantly standing to almost full height, their jagged edges gleam white against the particularly vibrant blue skies that one often finds around Norfolk's coast.

NORWICH CATHEDRAL PRIORY, NORWICH, NORFOLK

Second only to Salisbury in height, Norwich Cathedral's slender spire soars elegantly above a city containing over thirty medieval parish churches, dating back to a time when Norwich was a huddled collection of separate villages, their names remembered in the churches that survive them. That our religious heritage is enhanced by individual interpretation of architectural styles is perfectly reflected in the contrasting appearances of Norwich and Durham (see p. 56). No two buildings could be so visually diverse and yet both were conceived during the last decade of the eleventh century. The manner in which a church nave has been designed and built tends to set the tone for the entire building: Norwich creates a more subtle effect than its northern contemporary by placing less emphasis on huge supporting pillars, further reducing the impression of power by attaching additional slender columns to them. Founded in 1095 by Bishop Herbert Losinga, the cathedral became the East Anglian see in line with the Norman practice of locating them in larger towns. Two huge carved stones of great antiquity have been incorporated into the bishop's throne behind the high altar. They once formed part of a much earlier throne, probably dating back as far as the eighth century when the see was based at North Elmham. The chancel is more elaborate than is often

found in Norman churches, with beautifully proportioned rounded arches curving round to form an apse of great elegance. Perhaps the only slight disappointment is that the clerestory is from a later period, breaking up the symmetry of the Romanesque. However, the rebuilding was unavoidable as a collapsing spire, blown over by high winds, caused extensive damage early in the fourteenth century. A replacement was later destroyed by lightning, so the spire that adorns the cathedral today is the third version. Nature has not been the only cause of damage to the cathedral over the years, as civil unrest culminated in riots in 1272 in which the cloisters were burnt down. It took over a hundred and fifty years for them to be rebuilt, and one can readily recognize the passing of time in the changes of tracery design as work slowly progressed. One great treat that the monks were able to enjoy was the unusual addition of an enclosed upper level to the cloisters, enabling contemplation, writing and reading to be conducted in greater comfort during winter. Vaulting throughout the cathedral, including the cloisters, is adorned with hundreds of ornately carved bosses depicting biblical scenes in quite remarkable detail. The examples running round the cloister can be studied with the naked eye, while those in the nave require the help of magnifying mirror trolleys that have been thoughtfully provided.

TEWKESBURY ABBEY, TEWKESBURY, GLOUCESTERSHIRE

St Mary the Virgin is the most glorious of parish churches, a cathedral in all but name, rescued from the destructive hands of Henry VIII by the collective pride of Tewkesbury's inhabitants and the sum of £453, the cost of buying it intact at the Dissolution. It would be easy to get carried away with superlatives when describing the church, but most would be justified as there is so much craftsmanship and architectural detail to admire.

Norman work is of the highest quality, quite literally in the tower's case, as it is the tallest surviving example in the country – 132 feet high and 46 feet square, embellished with pronounced arcading. Completed in 1150, it would have provided a perfect vantage point from which to observe the Battle of Tewkesbury in 1471, one of the more bloody conflicts of the Wars of the Roses, resulting in a Yorkist victory over the Lancastrian forces and the death of the seventeen-year-old Prince of Wales. Accepting that defeat was inevitable, many Lancastrian troops fled to the perceived sanctuary of the church, but were cut down by a pursuing enemy, despite vain pleas for mercy from the abbot.

The nave is also a superb example of twelfth-century architecture. The solid pillars and undecorated rounded arches remain unaltered since completion, while the roof above them was replaced midway through the fourteenth century. The contrast between the complex lierne-vaulting and the stark simplicity of Norman stonework provides a visually appealing combination. Tewkesbury's other twelfth-century masterpiece is the huge, sixfold, recessed arch framing the west window, 65 feet high and perfectly carved in golden Cotswold limestone.

In contrast to the nave, the chancel was remodelled in the Decorated style, and has a much lighter atmosphere thanks largely to the extra light flooding in through the set of delicate traceried windows, some of which still contain original fourteenth-century stained glass. Encircling the chancel is a collection of medieval monuments and chantries, second only to those in Westminster Abbey (see p. 26). The Beauchamp chantry stands out as a stunning expression of Perpendicular architecture, and another chantry, dedicated to Hugh Despenser, has the unique detail of the kneeling knight on its roof, facing towards the altar. The Despenser family was one of the abbey's greatest patrons, and several other members are also remembered in monumental form.

A further chantry belongs to the abbey's founder, Robert Fitz Hamon, and other monuments radiate around behind the high altar. One to Abbot Wakeman is possibly not suitable for close inspection by the squeamish: above the tomb, a skeletal corpse is covered in 'creepy-crawlies', including a beetle, a worm, a snake and a mouse. Ashes to ashes?

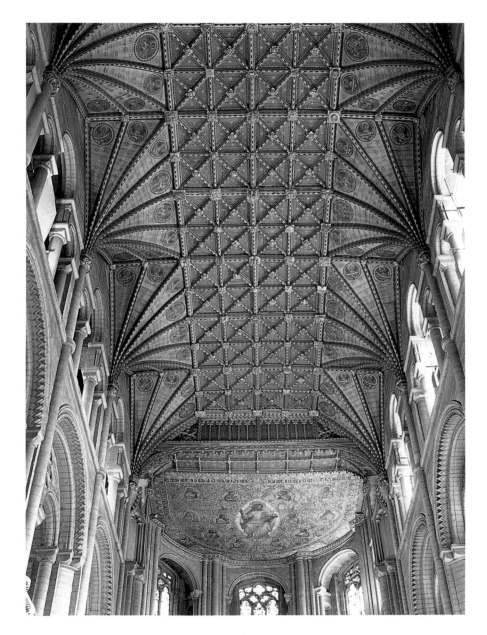

PETERBOROUGH CATHEDRAL ABBEY, PETERBOROUGH, CAMBRIDGESHIRE

It is depressing to see one of England's finest Romanesque churches almost totally engulfed by the concrete, brick and glass of Peterborough's modern shopping precincts. If only the cathedral had a landmark spire similar to Norwich instead of its rather squat tower, navigation towards the city centre through a confusing sprawl of industrial and urban development might be much easier. Henry VIII re-founded the abbey as one of his new Reformation cathedrals, probably out of political and geographical expedience rather than a sentimental desire to conserve the resting place of his divorced first wife, Catherine of Aragon, who died locally at Kimbolton in 1536 and was buried here to avoid the expense of a lavish funeral at St Paul's in London. There was another royal interment fifty years later when Mary, Queen of Scots was laid to rest after her execution at Fotheringhay, although her body was later transferred to Westminster Abbey by her son James I during his reign on the English throne. Formally known as Medeshamstede, Peterborough acquired its name from the monastery dedicated to St Peter, founded in 996 by Aethelwold, Bishop of Winchester. Those original Saxon buildings were destroyed by fire in 1116, and work on the present cathedral began some two years later, continuing well into the thirteenth

century. Most of the monastic buildings from that period have largely disappeared, although the current Deanery and Bishop's Palace both have surviving medieval features incorporated into solid Victorian restoration. The imposing west front is dominated by three 85-foot-high arches, pointed in the Early English style rather than the rounded Romanesque of the interior. Late afternoon is the time to enjoy that part of the exterior, when the sun's low angle highlights every carved detail on the mellow Barnack limestone in sharp relief. Peterborough is famed for its original painted nave ceiling, dating back to 1220 and decorated with human, animal and even grotesque figures among the geometric patterns. Even more lavishly coloured is the fifteenth-century presbytery ceiling, also of wood and ideally framed by the descending rows of clerestory, triforium and arcade, combined into a perfect symmetry of decorated arches, pillars and columns. One of the most intriguing monuments in the cathedral is dedicated to Robert Scarlett, the gravedigger responsible for the royal burials of Catherine and Mary, who died in 1594 at the remarkable age of ninety-eight. A committee charged with raising over £7 million for vital repairs to the building's ailing fabric targeted local businesses by asking for pledges of the curious sum of £1,721 each, being the abbey's annual income prior to its dissolution in 1539.

St Bees Priory, St Bees, Cumbria

Medieval legend attributes the origins of this site to Bega, an Irish girl who fled her homeland when faced with a forced marriage to a Viking chieftain. Having survived a shipwreck and been washed ashore on this isolated stretch of coast south of Whitehaven, Bega lived as a hermit, establishing a line of Christian worship unbroken since her arrival, possibly as early as 900.

The Norman Conquest took time to reach this far-flung corner of England, and although William le Meschin, Lord of Egremont, founded a small monastery at St Bees in 1120, it was not until some thirty years later that work began on the priory church. Monks from the prosperous Benedictine house of St Mary in York were invited to run St Bees, exchanging city life for the bracing Cumbrian seaside. Few traces of their domestic buildings remain, but one need only look across the road to St Bees School, founded less than fifty years after the Dissolution, to discover what became of the redundant stone. Framing the church's west door is a recessed Norman arch, an outstanding example of twelfth-century zigzag decoration. It is flanked by pillars and capitals that have not weathered so well, as the carved figures of grotesque mythical creatures have eroded into images which are far less likely to invade one's dreams.

Iona Abbey, Iona, Strathclyde, Scotland

This tiny island was one of the springboards from which Celtic Christianity was launched across northern England. Separated from the western shores of its more rugged neighbour Mull, Iona was where St Columba established his influential monastery in the sixth century, sending out missionaries such as Aidan to convert the pagan masses on the mainland.

Columba's reputation spread throughout Scotland, and Iona soon became established as a place of pilgrimage for those seeking knowledge and spiritual guidance. It is reputed that forty-eight ancient Scottish kings are buried here, culminating in 1040 with Duncan, who was allegedly murdered by Macbeth.

A Benedictine monastery was established during the thirteenth century and forms the nucleus of the restored church and ancillary buildings that dominate the delightful coastline of rocky coves and silver sands. The restored abbey is surrounded by several ancient Celtic crosses, carved with complex designs and symbols, but the most ancient example, St Oran's Cross, is preserved in the small island museum. Columba's ideals have not been forgotten as Iona is once more a place of retreat; if there is one place in Britain where one should be able to find an inner peace, it must surely be here.

THE AUGUSTINIANS

CHAPTER HOUSE

The chapter house of an abbey or priory was the second most important building after the church and was traditionally located in the cloister's east range. The chapter house was where the monastery's daily business was conducted at a morning meeting attended by all the brothers and presided over by the prior or abbot. It derived its name from the practice of beginning each meeting with a reading of a chapter from the Rule of St Benedict, after which other matters might include confessions and meting out appropriate punishments, the allocation of labour and any other affairs that affected the community as a whole.

Because of its status within a monastery, the chapter house was often built in a more elaborate style than other communal buildings. One of the most outstanding surviving examples is in Bristol Cathedral (see p. 94). Although there are seating allocations round the walls for up to forty people, it is unlikely that the number of canons in residence here would ever have reached that total.

The walls and vaulted ceiling feature an impressive display of pure Norman decoration at its most ebullient, including zigzag friezes and interlinked blind arcading, mostly untouched since the chapter house's completion towards the end of the twelfth century.

THE AUGUSTINIANS did not derive their name from the eponymous missionary responsible for reintroducing Christianity to England in 597, but modelled their order on the writings and instruction offered to a newly established religious foundation in fifth-century North Africa by St Augustine, Bishop of Hippo.

The Augustinian canons were not strictly a monastic order in the manner of Benedictines or Cistercians, although their doctrine did adopt numerous aspects of those rules laid down by St Benedict relating to appropriate conduct and management of religious houses. The canons lived in communities and in many respects adhered to the pattern of life one would have expected to find in any other monastery – devoting several hours of each day to worship, interspersed with work in the cloister and necessary manual labour.

What set the canons apart was their contact with the outside world, not only by venturing out into the towns and villages to preach, but also by welcoming the local population into their church for services. Many surviving Augustinian houses are distinguished by larger-than-average naves, specifically designed to house increased congregations.

Non-monastic churches, minsters and cathedrals had long been administered by groups of secular clerks, or canons, loosely based on a communal system but with fairly relaxed attitudes towards discipline. Many of them were married, and some priors and senior canons lived rather comfortably in separate houses.

It was groups such as these that Dunstan sought to replace with Benedictine monks during his drive to revive English monasticism after its decline following the Viking onslaughts of the ninth century. Once Augustinians became part of the religious fabric of England, they too replaced the secular incumbents in many ailing foundations.

Although not directly under any form of papal control, canons in Europe were being encouraged to follow monastic guidelines more closely, particularly in respect of poverty and chastity (one wonders just how readily such creature comforts were renounced). A suitable set of rules was eventually formulated, adopting a less dogmatic approach to matters such as length of services, diet and other aspects rigorously adhered to by Benedictine communities.

The Augustinians were an accepted order on the Continent long before the Norman Conquest but were not introduced into England until around 1100. Their first house was St

Botulph's in Colchester, where they replaced the existing clergy. Henry I and Queen Matilda were largely responsible for establishing new Augustinian houses in England, spread over a wide area that included Launceston in Cornwall, Cirencester, London and Oxford.

The Austin canons, as the order was called in England, were also known as the 'black canons' after the colour of the outer cloaks worn when they were out in public away from the priories – they were often seconded as parish priests in neighbouring villages.

Because of their accessibility and willingness to be integrated into life outside the cloister, the Austins became an accepted part of society and were well supported in many regions, although the majority of their houses were never sufficiently wealthy to achieve abbatial rank and it was not uncommon to find establishments populated by ten or fewer canons.

Despite its lack of rich endowments, the Austin movement's popularity resulted in a rapid escalation of new houses, a momentum that led to a total of around a hundred and seventy, plus twenty-three separate nunneries, by the time of the Dissolution.

Most Augustinian houses fell under the jurisdiction of the local bishop, who carried out annual inspections where possible to determine whether the establishment was being run in an appropriate manner and to hear grievances and complaints from the canons. There were numerous houses where the bishop himself might have been the complainant, not least at Dorchester Abbey (see p. 93) where reputedly there was nightly entertaining of the opposite sex on a regular (or more probably irregular) basis, the prior himself allegedly not immune to such secular pleasures.

Architecturally, the Austin presence covered a wide spectrum and, unlike orders such as the Cistercians, could never really be typified by the style either of its churches or associated domestic buildings, although in most instances the conventional claustral layout was followed.

Augustinians may have possessed fewer of the great churches than other orders, but they were in charge of one of the country's most important places of pilgrimage, Our Lady of Walsingham, where a priory was founded in 1169. Most medieval monarchs made the journey to Walsingham, and even Henry VIII left his shoes in the Slipper Chapel to walk the last mile barefoot, although that was several years before his attitude towards the monasteries underwent a substantial reappraisal.

LLANTHONY PRIORY, NR ABERGAVENNY, GWENT, WALES

Even Lancelot 'Capability' Brown, the eighteenth-century landscape gardener, would be hard-pressed to improve on nature's raw state as presented in the beautiful Honddu Valley, which runs parallel with Offa's Dyke and the English border on the Black Mountains' eastern flank.

The legend of Llanthony's foundation centres around William de Lacy, a Norman knight who, while out hunting in the area towards the end of the eleventh century, took shelter in an ancient chapel dedicated to St David. There he underwent a 'road to Damascus' experience that resulted in him abandoning all worldly goods to live there as a hermit in religious study and contemplation. He was initially joined in his devotions by a priest named Ersinius, and, soon after, other supporters swelled the community as word spread round the region.

A church and priory of Augustinian canons was finally established in 1118, having been given a degree of financial stability and independence through endowments from one of William's relatives, Hugh de Lacy. Ersinius became first prior of Llanthony, but the tranquillity was relatively short-lived. Following the death of Henry I, a Welsh uprising sought to drive all vestiges of the Norman Conquest from Welsh soil. The priory was abandoned by almost all the canons for fifty years;

the majority of them moved to the safety of a new foundation near Gloucester, appropriately named Llanthony Secunda.

Those parts of the church and priory that survive today date from a building programme undertaken during the latter part of the twelfth and early decades of the thirteenth centuries, employing a particularly austere Transitional style of architecture that blends harmoniously with such wild and lonely surroundings. The north aisle arcade survives intact to the crossing tower, on which can be traced the line of the nave's roof.

Llanthony did not escape harm, suffering at the hands of both English and Welsh forces, notably during the uprising led by Owen Glendower at the turn of the fifteenth century. The priory never fully recovered from the damage inflicted during those attacks and stumbled onwards in financial decline until the Dissolution, at which time its occupants had dwindled to a prior and four canons.

Since that time, a succession of owners, perhaps inspired by artistic trends such as the Picturesque movement, have sought to harness Llanthony's natural charms for their own pleasures. Poet Walter Savage Landor's grandiose plans for transforming the ruins and surrounding countryside into a model estate were thwarted by unco-operative locals, unimpressed by such a scheme. Disenchanted and considerably poorer, Landor moved abroad where he reduced his Welsh experiences to an ironic

couplet: 'I loved thee by thy streams of yore/ By distant streams, I love thee more.'

The priory has long been converted into a hotel, fashioned out of the western tower and adjoining buildings, enabling guests to savour the atmosphere of an isolated priory but with the benefit of more creature comforts than those available to its original residents.

While many nineteenth-century visitors extolled the romantic experience of staying among the ruins, the legendary Victorian Welsh diarist, Rev. Francis Kilvert, bemoaned such organized tourism, and after one visit was moved to write, ' If there is one thing more hateful than another, it is being told what to admire and have objects pointed out to one with a stick.' Kilvert's comments might have been prejudiced by the fact that, after a long mountain walk, his lunch was considerably delayed by the visiting party monopolizing the hotel dining room.

However, despite the modern-day creation of a car park and discreetly sited public conveniences, the reverend gentleman can rest assured that 'stick pointing' has still not taken off in a big way at Llanthony and the majority of tourists remain unorganized.

HEXHAM ABBEY, HEXHAM, NORTHUMBERLAND

A reminder of Hexham's monastic tradition survives in the present church's south transept, where the monks' night stair descends from what was once their dormitory. The stair now features on special occasions, used as a candlelit processional by the abbey choir, and has become something of a tourist attraction. Very little imagination is required to turn the clock back a few centuries to visualize the canons making their way down into an almost pitch-black void for the 2 a.m. office of lauds, a darkness relieved only by shallow pools of light cast from spluttering candles.

This feature is unusual as access to the church was commonly via external stairs leading down into the cloister and entry through the east processional door, a route originally followed at Hexham until the revised layout. It must have come as a welcome relief for the monks no longer to have to brave the elements, but on reflection, maybe a cold blast of wind on the face might have helped dispel further thoughts of sleep. Each stone on the stairs has been unevenly eroded by the tread of countless feet over the centuries. Even closer inspection will reveal traces of lead in places, a reminder of more turbulent times when the Scots set fire to the abbey during a raid in 1296, causing molten lead to drip down from the burning church roof. That particular attack was both cruel and destructive, as the intruders locked

many novices into a storeroom that was then deliberately set alight. The nave was so badly damaged it had to be bricked off and was only rebuilt at the start of the twentieth century.

Hexham's abbey church is renowned for its seventh-century Saxon crypt, acknowledged as the finest of the six known surviving examples in England and certainly one of the most moving and evocative remnants of early Christianity. Its existence was discovered purely by accident in 1725 during digging operations for the foundations of a huge buttress to support the tower. Medieval church records made no reference to the crypt, originally part of Wilfred's Saxon cathedral that first occupied the site, so it had lain undisturbed beneath the earth and rubble of the abbey's ruined nave.

The stones used in its construction bear Roman inscriptions and decoration, having originally formed part of the nearby Roman fort of Corstopium, modern-day Corbridge. No daylight pierces the crypt's gloom, and as one stoops beneath the barrel-vaulted chamber, it would come as no great surprise to be confronted by the spectre of an ancient monk, still zealously guarding the saintly relics once housed in the crypt.

GUISBOROUGH PRIORY, GUISBOROUGH, CLEVELAND

There may not be much of Guisborough Priory left, but that which survives cannot fail to impress. The magnificent east end of the church stands to its full original height of around 97 feet, and its visual impact has been enhanced by the removal of a wall beneath the huge central window. Guisborough was initially well endowed, having been founded around 1120 by Robert de Brus, a wealthy baron whose brother William became first prior. It is no coincidence that their name bears an uncanny resemblance to that of one of Scotland's most famous kings, Robert Bruce, as he was indeed a descendant of William. Having prospered throughout the twelfth century, the monks decided to rebuild their monastery completely, a task that took most of the following century at great expense. Final touches were being applied to the new church when an act of carelessness by a craftsman resulted in a catastrophic fire that virtually gutted the building. Reconstruction began in 1289 and it is the remains of the church from that era that grace the site today. Guisborough was just one of many north country monasteries to suffer at the hands of Scottish raiders during the early fourteenth century following Bruce's comprehensive victory over the English at Bannockburn in 1314. It seems ironic that his countrymen were looting and despoiling a religious house established by their beloved king's ancestors.

BOLTON PRIORY, NR SKIPTON, NORTH YORKSHIRE

Countless artists and poets have travelled to this most beautiful part of Yorkshire in search of inspiration and few have left Wharfedale unrewarded, not least J. M. W. Turner whose watercolours perfectly capture the romantic atmosphere generated by the priory's tree-lined riverside setting, picturesquely framed against a backdrop of distant hills. The gaunt outline of the roofless chancel with its huge east window still towers nobly over the swirling River Wharfe below, perhaps creating the impression when viewed from a distance that Bolton is ruined throughout. On closer inspection, the nave is revealed to be far from redundant; indeed, it still functions as the parish church much as it has done for centuries, with a neatly fenced graveyard spreading down towards the river's edge. Upon its foundation in 1120, the priory was first established at Embsay, some four miles away from the present site, and although the surroundings of that area are pleasant enough, one suspects that significantly fewer canvasses, poems and essays would have been produced in praise of the priory had it remained there. The land surrounding Embsay became barren and unworkable, necessitating the move to a more fertile location. Despite being neither large nor wealthy, Bolton was nevertheless subjected to numerous attacks by Scottish raiders during forays south. The most severe was early in the

fourteenth century and caused severe structural damage and the temporary abandonment of the site by many of the terrified canons. When peace descended once again on Wharfedale, the vandalized chancel was rebuilt in the Decorated style, although traces of earlier Norman work were retained, notably sections of round-headed blind arcading. Although no monastic buildings survive above ground, their size and original layout can be traced through exposed foundations of the claustral ranges, evidence that includes the outline of an unusual octagonal chapter house, whose total disappearance is a cause of great sadness. Visitors to the parish church may be slightly puzzled by the presence of a large square entrance porch, obscuring much of the exquisite Early English west front. In 1520 work had begun on a tower that, judging by the size and elaborate style of its base, would have been a very grand structure, but further progress was halted by the unwelcome arrival of Henry VIII's Commissioners, from whom the Cavendish family (subsequently Dukes of Devonshire) acquired the property after the Dissolution. During dry summer months when the river's level subsides, a large sandy beach is exposed on the bank opposite the ruins. Shaded by overhanging trees, it forms one of the most perfect picnic sites one could ever hope to find.

KIRKHAM PRIORY, NR MALTON, NORTH YORKSHIRE

First established in 1120, the ruins of Kirkham Priory are scattered alongside the gently meandering River Derwent, a few miles to the south of Malton. Beyond the far bank a steep escarpment climbs to join the busy main road linking York and the seaside resort of Scarborough. Thankfully, however, the tree-lined slopes help obliterate traffic noise and the site's tranquillity is broken only by an occasional passing train, railway engineers having chosen to follow the easier terrain carved out by the river. A bridle path running along the escarpment edge overlooking the site offers a comprehensive aerial view, particularly useful in deciphering the monastery's layout as many buildings have been reduced to foundation wall level.

Kirkham was the first of three monasteries to be established by Walter l'Espec, Lord of Helmsley, although perhaps he is better remembered for his second foundation, the great Cistercian abbey at Rievaulx (see p. 112), some ten years later. It was inevitable that his first religious house would be for Augustinians as the order had the personal patronage of Henry I, the same monarch responsible for granting both lands and title to l'Espec.

Given its remoteness and river setting, one could easily assume that Kirkham was a typical site favoured by Cistercians, and at one stage it nearly did change its allegiance to Cîteaux, going so far as to have appropriate

documents drawn up. The main protagonist was Prior Waltheof, although records show he did not enjoy universal support among the community. The situation was resolved by his departure to join the 'white monks' at neighbouring Rievaulx, and whatever remaining internal differences existed over doctrine were obviously resolved as Kirkham ultimately remained loyal to the creed of St Augustine.

Excavations have traced the origins of three churches, based on the initial simple cruciform building dating from about ten years after the priory's foundation. The final version constructed during the thirteenth century was 300 feet long, although a planned tower was never added. Kirkham's outstanding surviving feature is its Decorated-style, late thirteenth-century gatehouse, adorned with carvings depicting George and the Dragon, David and Goliath, coats of arms and, set in niches directly above the rib-vaulted arched entrance, figures of Christ, St Philip and St Bartholomew.

The aesthetic balance of the gatehouse is greatly enhanced by the window's elaborately embellished tracery that has remained intact, contributing to the façade's beauty. Above the archway itself, heraldic shields bear the arms of England, l'Espec and other noble families including the de Roos, later patrons of the priory whose burial ground was beneath the church's chancel.

CHRIST CHURCH CATHEDRAL, ST FRIDESWIDE'S PRIORY, OXFORD, OXFORDSHIRE

One might have expected the cathedral of such an historic city as Oxford to occupy a prominent position, but the entrance to Christ Church Cathedral could readily be mistaken for one of the college buildings that flank the vast quadrangle known as Tom Quad. It is quite likely that many of the tourists who descend on Oxford will have 'done' Christ Church without realizing they have actually been inside a cathedral, not merely another chapel.

St Frideswide was the head of a nunnery here in the eighth century, long before Oxford itself existed, but no traces of that establishment remain. The priory for Augustinian canons served by the present church was founded by Henry I in 1122. University colleges had existed in Oxford since early in the thirteenth century, but in 1524 Cardinal Wolsey decided to surpass them all by creating his own lavishly endowed institution, suppressing St Frideswide's Priory by means of a Papal petition.

The cardinal's fall from grace in 1529 is well documented and Henry VIII's subsequent intervention in his ambitious scheme may well have prevented demolition of the original priory church to make way for a new chapel. Several bays of the nave, amounting to some 50 feet, had already been lost to accommodate Tom Quad, but despite those alterations, the king elected to retain the truncated building,

initially as the college chapel before eventually designating it a cathedral in 1546, after Oxford was made a diocese. Typical Norman architecture prevails in the nave, leading towards tall, rounded crossing arches that perfectly frame the contrasting riot of lierne vaulting over the choir, resembling the writhing network of tendrils of an exotic plant. Many of the original monastic buildings have either been demolished or incorporated into the college, one notable survivor being the thirteenth-century chapter house containing Early English lancets and a rib-vaulted ceiling adorned with highly decorated bosses. During the English Civil War midway through the seventeenth century, Charles I made Oxford his headquarters, with Christ Church as his personal base. That period in the cathedral's history is recalled in some of the monuments to the Cavaliers who died fighting for the Royalist cause. Christ Church boasts an enviable collection of stained glass in contrasting styles, ranging from nineteenth-century Pre-Raphaelite windows by Burne-Jones to medieval glass from the fourteenth century in St Lucy's chapel. The Becket window contains one particular segment that highlights the saint's martyrdom, a portrayal that should have been destroyed at the Dissolution, along with all other images of Thomas à Becket. This example survived because a fragment of plain glass was inserted to replace the bishop's face, thereby escaping detection.

HAUGHMOND ABBEY, NR SHREWSBURY, SHROPSHIRE

Dedicated to St John the Evangelist, Haughmond was a rarity among Augustinian monasteries in achieving abbatial status, having been initially established as a priory during the 1130s by William Fitzalan of Clun. Archaeological evidence shows traces of an original smaller church on the site occupied by its larger successor, which was probably erected when extensive rebuilding took place late in the twelfth century, coinciding with Haughmond's increased status. Unfortunately, nothing of the abbey church survives, but the site is architecturally and historically important in other respects.

From its elevated position on a steep hillside, the abbey enjoys sweeping views across Shrewsbury to the Welsh border hills, but the pronounced absence of level ground meant that the customary monastic layout could not be followed. The usual east–west progression of buildings had to be abandoned in favour of laying out the site on a north–south axis, using a rare double cloister system: those buildings normally found on the east side were established further to the south, notably the infirmary and abbot's lodging. Haughmond's infirmary seems to have been a rather grand building by monastic standards, judging by what remains. One row of elegant twin-light windows is augmented by an even larger opening in the west wall, flanked by twin turrets. One imagines there might have been no shortage of potential

patients seeking pampering during those winter months when icy gales whipped across the plain, buffeting Haughmond's exposed position. Standing amid the gleaming stone walls and neatly trimmed grass, it is hard to imagine that parts of the site were still occupied by farm buildings and dwellings before excavations began early in the twentieth century.

Following the Dissolution, the abbot's hall and lodging were converted into a mansion, subsequently destroyed a century later during the Civil War. Haughmond was acquired by new owners for domestic and agricultural use early in the eighteenth century, but fortunately they left most of the monastic remains intact.

Even though the abbot's lodging had been modified and improved during post-Dissolution conversion, it is easy to see that the building still represented a far more luxurious form of accommodation than that enjoyed (or not) by the canons. It might also be reasonable to assume that meals of varying quality were prepared in the kitchens located midway between the abbot's hall and communal frater.

The west-facing chapter house entrance from the cloister is a typically splendid Norman affair comprising three deeply recessed arches, linked by slender columns. In complete contrast, the eastern aspect now possesses a sixteenth-century bay window, a legacy of the later amendments.

JEDBURGH ABBEY, JEDBURGH, BORDERS, SCOTLAND

Jedburgh's abbey church, roofless but standing proudly to its full height, dominates the scanty remains of the monastic buildings descending in stepped layers to the north bank of Jed Water. Directly opposite the abbey, a large car park and picnic area offers a perfect vantage point from which one can more fully appreciate the graceful lines of windows and arches that pierce the nave walls, although the rather squat tower, rebuilt without its spire in the sixteenth century, seems somehow out of proportion amid such architectural finesse. Perhaps the most surprising thing about the abbey is its continued existence in such a complete state when one considers how many times it was sacked and burnt during the border region's turbulent history. In much the same way that northern English abbeys and churches fell prey to marauding Scots, Jedburgh suffered reciprocal treatment at the hands of English forces, the town having had the misfortune to be located only a few miles north of the border on the only main route north through the bleak mass of the Cheviot Hills. King David I of Scotland and John, Bishop of Glasgow, were jointly responsible for Jedburgh's original foundation as a priory in 1138, its status raised to that of an abbey a few years later. It does seem extraordinary that such a lavish establishment should have been set up so close to England, given the less than cordial relationship that existed between

the two nations for much of the Middle Ages. However, it may well be that David used Jedburgh's proximity to England to prove that Scotland was perfectly capable of managing its own religious affairs and should not have been under the jurisdiction of the Archbishop of York. In common with many other large abbey churches, Jedburgh features work from more than one architectural style and is considered to be a particularly fine example of the Transitional, that period of building during the late twelfth and early thirteenth centuries when the heavy Romanesque pillars and rounded, zigzag decorated arches of the Romanesque began to be replaced by the lighter, pointed arches, windows and doorways of the Gothic periods that followed. Times of stability and peace in the abbey's history were few and far between, so that by the time of the Reformation in 1560, most of the buildings were dilapidated, apart from an area beneath the tower crossing that was used for worship. Eventually, this too proved unsound and a new parish church was fashioned from the western end of the nave in 1671, remaining in use until the latter part of the nineteenth century when a new church was built elsewhere in the town.

THORNTON ABBEY, NR IMMINGHAM, LINCOLNSHIRE

It seems somehow unfair that this most impressive and beautiful example of a monastic gatehouse should be marooned in such an unsympathetic environment. Thornton Abbey deserves to be set in a leafy idyll, surrounded by pastoral beauty; instead, its horizon is filled with the visual debris of the oil refineries, chemical works and docks that have become established along the River Humber's desolate south shore. Remains of the church and other buildings are sparse, although two elegantly decorated sections of the octagonal chapter house survive, providing an insight into just how opulent and well endowed the abbey must have been. Fortunately, the gatehouse is virtually intact and is a quite extraordinary piece of work. Although stone has been used in its construction, the predominant material is brick, probably ferried across the Humber from Hull, one of the few known brickmaking centres in the fourteenth century. Perhaps the most surprising aspect of the gatehouse is its defensive nature, accessible only by bridge across a moat and with a frontage liberally pierced with arrow slits. One explanation for the presence of these slits might be that building took place around the time of the ultimately unsuccessful Peasants' Revolt of 1381 led by Wat Tyler, an uprising that may well have caused anxiety to the abbot of a rich but isolated abbey.

DORCHESTER ABBEY, DORCHESTER, OXFORDSHIRE

Recognized as one of England's oldest Christian foundations, Dorchester was originally the see of a vast Saxon diocese, given to St Birinus by one of his most powerful converts, King Cyngelis of Wessex.

An Augustinian abbey replaced the cathedral in 1170, and although most of the monastic buildings were destroyed at the Dissolution, the church was bought for the community by a rich merchant named Richard Beauforest. The Norman church is represented by the nave's north wall, but the additions from later periods are those that contribute so much to Dorchester's character.

Dating from the fourteenth-century Decorated period, the Jesse window is a work of extraordinary complexity – intricately carved stone and stained glass mingle to form a 'family tree' depicting Christ's descent from Jesse, father of King David.

One of Dorchester's other great treasures is the thirteenth-century tomb effigy of a Crusader knight, Sir John Holcombe, whose body is partially twisted with hand on sword in anticipation of confronting an unseen foe, possibly even death itself. A curious epitaph lies in the south aisle where a black stone tablet dedicated to Mrs Sarah Fletcher, who died in 1799, informs us that she was 'a martyr to excessive sensibility'– not the commonest of complaints.

BRISTOL CATHEDRAL ABBEY, BRISTOL, AVON

Unlike several of its medieval counterparts, Bristol Cathedral is sited a short distance away from city centre bustle and traffic, allowing it to retain some of the tranquil atmosphere associated with a monastic past extending back to 1140 when the abbey was founded by Robert FitzHardinge, Provost of Bristol. Fortunately, Bristol was one of the six monasteries designated as cathedrals by Henry VIII at the Dissolution, thereby preserving one of the most remarkable examples of church building in England. The early fourteenth-century chancel, conceived by Abbot Knowle, draws admiration from both lay visitors and architects alike. Referred to as a 'hall-church', St Augustine's is remarkable for the aisles that rise to the same height as the chancel, creating one vast pillared area, filled with light and blessed with greatly enhanced acoustics. The successful accomplishment of this particular design cannot be underestimated in technical terms and, at the time of completion, it was conceptually way ahead of other churches constructed in both England and Europe. As there are no external flying buttresses providing support, the downward thrust of the roof is absorbed by a combination of vaulting, strong pillars and an ingenious system of horizontal bridges running across the aisle arches, enabling a balanced transfer of weight to the outside walls. Four chapels flank the chancel and, unusually, two of them are

dedicated to the Virgin Mary. Lady chapels are customarily located behind the high altar, and the later of the two, built in 1298, occupies that position; the other, which is some fifty years older and referred to as the Elder Lady Chapel, is to the east of the north transept. It actually stood as a separate entity during construction of the cathedral, being joined on later by the formation of two arches in its southern wall. Curiously, some of the chapel's intricate stone carvings are effigies of monkeys, one of which can be seen playing a set of bagpipes. This work is almost identical to similar examples in Wells Cathedral and is probably the trademark of one craftsman, a theory perhaps confirmed by a letter held in the British Museum from Abbot David of Bristol to his counterpart at Wells, requesting the services of a stonemason. Despite appearing to be no more than a narrow antechamber leading into the Berkeley chapel, the sacristy is in fact one of the most fascinating parts of the cathedral, with a rare skeleton-vaulted roof. Facing the entrance are three elegantly carved stone niches where preparation for Mass took place; the left hand one is the oven where the bread was baked, complete with a flue disappearing up into the wall. One can imagine how tantalizing the smell of freshly baked bread wafting through to the choir might have been to hungry monks on a cold winter's morning. The monks' chapter house remains virtually unaltered since its completion in 1165 and is an absolute delight. Entered

through a dark, three-bayed vestibule of interlinked arches, its walls have been adorned with a typically complex array of geometric Romanesque decoration. Many of the other surviving monastic buildings have been incorporated into the adjacent Cathedral School. One exception is the abbey gatehouse, the ground floor of which dates from the same period as the chapter house. Although eroded in parts and blackened with grime, it exhibits the same quality of stonework. Victorian architects have often been pilloried for their insensitive and overzealous restoration of many churches, but no praise is high enough for G. E. Street, who designed and constructed the present nave, its predecessor having been demolished after the Dissolution. His work both respects and mirrors the techniques used by Abbot Knowle, and, although built centuries apart, both segments of the abbey blend seamlessly together.

LILLESHALL ABBEY, NR NEWPORT, SHROPSHIRE

The richly decorated west entrance to Lilleshall Abbey's large red sandstone church comes alive in splashes of vibrant colour when touched by evening sunlight. Even more elaborately carved patterns can be found on the secluded processional entrance leading from the cloisters, now almost entirely shaded by the spreading foliage of giant ancient yew trees. Luckily, neither of these precious examples of Late Norman architecture suffered serious damage when besieged by Parliamentarian forces during the Civil War of the 1640s. From some time after the Dissolution, the abbey was owned by the Leveson family who subsequently converted the claustral buildings for domestic use, and it was Sir Richard Leveson, a staunch supporter of Charles I, who successfully defended the site for several weeks. The absence of a north transept in an otherwise fairly complete ruined church is explained by the fact that this was the entry point for Cromwell's forces. Although subsequently incorporated into the Augustinian order, the first occupants of Lilleshall were canons from a French abbey at Arrouaise, their doctrine originally embracing some of the more austere principles of the Cistercians. Centuries after the canons' departure, Lilleshall is once more a focus of total dedication even though the cloisters remain silent and deserted. Close by the abbey the large hall built by the Levesons now forms the core of the English National Sports Centre.

LANERCOST PRIORY, NR BRAMPTON, CUMBRIA

Being situated so close to the Scottish border, unfortified religious institutions such as Lanercost represented an easy source of plunder to the bands of Scottish raiders who terrorized northern England during the thirteenth and fourteenth centuries. Serious damage was inflicted during attacks in 1296 (the same incursion that led to the burning of Hexham, see p. 78), the following year by 'Braveheart' himself, William Wallace, and later by King David II in 1346. Effecting constant repairs was a costly business that caused serious financial problems for the canons despite the abbey having been well endowed at its foundation by Robert de Vaux in 1166. Large segments of their estates had to be sold to meet increasing debts, which left the abbey with an annual income of only about £80 in the sixteenth century. Probably one of the most difficult times in Lanercost's history was when Edward I and his royal entourage of around two hundred made a prolonged visit during the autumn and winter of 1306. The king had only intended to stay a few days while en route to Carlisle, but was taken ill and remained at the abbey until the following March. He made little further progress, eventually dying by the Solway Firth in July. Lanercost remains not only an impressive ruin but also a parish church, as the original abbey nave was restored and re-roofed, leaving tower, chancel and transepts open to the elements.

PRIORY CHURCH OF
ST MARY AND ST MICHAEL,
CARTMEL, CUMBRIA

Visitors to the delightful village of
Cartmel are usually surprised by the
disproportionately large parish church,
famous for its unusual lantern set
diagonally on top of the crossing tower.
The priory church originally served a
community of canons founded in 1188
by William Marshall, First Earl of
Pembroke, and was subsequently
retained intact for village use after the
Dissolution. Parishioners had
personally appealed to Henry VIII to be
allowed to keep their church, efforts
that met with greater success than those
Cartmel monks who paid with their
lives for joining the 'Pilgrimage of
Grace', a northern-based movement
against the Dissolution. The rebellion
was swiftly and ruthlessly put down by
the king, and many of the abbots, priors
and monks who had joined the
movement in a vain attempt to save
their beloved monasteries were executed.
Inside the church, although one's
attention is immediately drawn to the
four huge piers of the crossing that
support the tower, there is much else to
admire, such as carved misericords, an
even more intricately decorated wooden
screen and, affixed to the walls,
colourfully painted boards bearing the
Lord's Prayer, the Ten Commandments
and the Creed, all meticulously handwritten in Gothic script. A gatehouse in
one corner of the tiny market square is
the only other surviving trace of the
original conventual buildings.

WHITELADIES PRIORY,
NR TONG, SHROPSHIRE

Founded for Augustinian canonesses
around the twelfth century,
Whiteladies' name was derived from the
pale, undyed woollen garments worn by
its occupants. All that now remains of
the priory is the humble church and it is
difficult to imagine that this site played
a leading role in one of English history's
great folklore events, Charles II's escape
from Cromwell's soldiers after defeat at
the Battle of Worcester in 1651 by
hiding in the now-famous oak tree near
Boscobel House.

Whiteladies had been owned by a
succession of Catholic families after the
Dissolution, who lived in a timber-
framed house surrounded by a walled
garden on the site, and it was here that
Charles first sought refuge. A painting
by Robert Streeter, dated 1670, depicts
the king's flight, aided by his close
friend William Penderel. The royal
fugitive is portrayed furtively sneaking
from a rear entrance while his entourage
gallops away from the front, a
subterfuge enabling Charles to head
towards Boscobel House and his
celebrated rendezvous with the
protective oak.

Penderel's burial stone is in the chancel
of Whiteladies, the walls of which are
also sadly adorned in part by modern
graffiti detailing secular activities that
would have made the canonesses blush;
but even that cannot detract from the
simple beauty of this historic site.

WOODSPRING PRIORY, NR WESTON-SUPER-MARE, NORTH SOMERSET

Despite Woodspring Priory's proximity to the seaside resort of Weston-Super-Mare, its isolated location on the sparsely populated coastal fringes to the north make it difficult to locate. Navigational perseverance is recommended as there is much to admire at Woodspring, part of which has been restored by the Landmark Trust, which makes it available to rent for holidays. Accommodation occupies part of the nave, but the crossing and infirmary are open to visitors, as is a delightful museum room, housing a collection of books, documents and artefacts relating to Woodspring's history and restoration.

The priory was founded in 1210 by William de Courtenay, whose grandfather was one of the infamous 'Canterbury Four' responsible for the murder of Thomas à Becket in Canterbury Cathedral (see p. 44). De Courtenay's motives for establishing this house of Victorine Augustinian canons are unclear, but it would be quite reasonable to assume it was an act of family atonement, as the chosen patron saint of the foundation was St Thomas the Martyr.

Rising ground behind the priory offers a good vantage point from which to study the compactly grouped buildings *in situ*; the original range was augmented slightly to create a farm after the Dissolution.

MICHELHAM PRIORY, NR HAILSHAM, EAST SUSSEX

The River Cuckmere flows into the English Channel at a point where the South Downs end at the Seven Sisters, a dramatic, scalloped line of soaring white chalk cliffs culminating in Beachy Head. Further upstream in more tranquil surroundings, the river has been diverted to feed the large moat surrounding Michelham Priory, which covers an area of six-and-a-half acres, making it one of the largest surviving examples in England.

Founded for Augustinian canons in 1229, Michelham was seemingly unremarkable in terms of size or wealth and yet was deemed worthy of protection on all sides by a moat more appropriate to a medieval fortress. Sole access is over a bridge guarded by a splendid late fourteenth-century gatehouse.

Following the Dissolution, most of the priory was destroyed, leaving only the refectory and adjoining buildings, which were incorporated into a Tudor manor house. The site originally occupied by the church has been excavated to reveal its outline, but apart from the gatehouse, all other traces of monastic inhabitation have disappeared. The whole site is owned and managed by the Sussex Archaeological Trust, which has beautifully converted the house into a museum, while the priory grounds now house a weatherboarded barn surrounded by ancient farming paraphernalia.

THE CISTERCIANS

FOUNTAINS ABBEY

The ruins of Fountains Abbey (see p. 116) are remarkable for the amount that has survived intact, most notably the number of domestic buildings that remain above ground and in such good condition. This is all the more surprising when one remembers that similar sites were customarily treated as ready-made stone quarries after the Dissolution.

Fountain's remoteness was probably a major deterrent to potential stone robbers, as transportation of its stone would have proved very costly and laborious. Most of the infirmary was in fact demolished, but the materials were only removed 650 feet and were used by Stephen Proctor to build the splendid Fountains Hall around the end of the sixteenth century.

The abbey ruins became the centre-piece of an ambitious landscaping scheme undertaken by the Aislabie family during the eighteenth century, which included water gardens, cascades and temples. These are all now combined in the magnificent Studley estate, owned by the National Trust and designated a World Heritage Site.

THE CISTERCIAN MOVEMENT was conceived out of the frustration and disenchantment felt by some Benedictine monks who considered that attitudes and behaviour in their own order had fallen significantly below the required standards laid out in the Rule of St Benedict. A group of monks from the French monastery of Molesme in Burgundy were the first to make their feelings known in a practical way. In 1098 they established a new community amid the solitude and peace of the forests around Cîteaux, whose Latin name was 'Cistercium'; it was from this name that the order derived its title.

Links with Molesme had not been severed with the specific intention of founding a new order. The monks merely desired to adhere more strictly to the Benedictine code, which had gradually been eroded by laziness, complacency and greed, particularly in abbeys near major towns where attention was easily diverted away from the psalter.

An English monk named Stephen Harding was one of the prime motivators of the new order and subsequently became abbot of Cîteaux, playing an important role in dictating how the movement should proceed. He was joined in 1111 by a monk named Bernard, who later established the second monastery at Clairvaux and became a key figure in Cistercian expansion during the early decades of the twelfth century.

Unlike Benedictine monasteries, which functioned independently of each other, the Cistercians regarded themselves as a united family, irrespective of an abbey's location. The new rules were expected to be universally observed, with each monastery conforming to exactly the same standards of liturgy, dress and lifestyle.

New abbeys were colonized by monks from existing monasteries, and the sense of a family relationship between them was summed up in the analogy of 'mother' and 'daughter' houses. To ensure that appropriate standards were maintained, each monastery was inspected annually by the mother house's abbot. On a wider scale, all abbots were required to attend an annual chapter meeting at Cîteaux to formulate new legislation for the order as a whole.

Cistercians were known as 'white monks' because of their habits of coarse, undyed sheep's wool, and the harshness of their environment matched that of their garments. Monasteries were built in remote locations; the buildings themselves were magnificent but architecturally austere, furnishings were basic with few adornments and, where other churches might use gold or silver for items such as candlesticks, Cistercians made do with iron. A vegetarian diet was mandatory and, although meals were taken communally, a strict observance of silence was broken only by the voice of the refectory scripture reader.

The first foundation in Britain was established in 1128, at Waverley in Surrey, followed during the early 1130s by the splendid abbeys of Rievaulx, Fountains and Tintern. The popularity of the newly evolved order was reflected in its rapid growth during the first half of the twelfth century – forty-six out of a final total of sixty-four monasteries had been founded by the time of King Stephen's death in 1154.

Cistercian rules forbade the acceptance of gifts other than land, which led to an agriculturally biased economy with abbeys owning vast acreages, either in the immediate vicinity or in outlying districts known as 'granges'. Because a large number of Cistercian houses were in the wilder parts of Britain, sheep farming became the main source of income. Some of the larger abbeys became renowned for the size of their flocks, some of which numbered several thousand, generating huge revenues from the lucrative medieval wool trade.

To enable the monks to devote adequate time to prayer, worship and work in the cloister, the Cistercians established the practice of using 'lay brothers' to manage their estates, tend flocks and perform other manual tasks. Mostly illiterate, the lay brothers had their own accommodation and refectory in the monastery but took lesser vows and attended fewer services.

There was never a shortage of new patrons anxious to support the order, but the land they wanted to donate was often already occupied by farms and villages. The monks' desire to retain such gifts led to the somewhat un-Christian practice of transforming the land into barren areas by simply evicting existing tenants and even demolishing unwanted settlements.

As time passed, lay brothers became less amenable to exploitation and fewer were recruited. This reduction in the labour force was exacerbated towards the end of the fourteenth century by the Black Death, which severely reduced the country's population. Deprived of their farm workers, the Cistercians were forced to become landlords and gather income from tithes and rents. By this process they gradually moved away from their puritanical ideals back towards the materialistic ways they had originally been founded to avoid.

Post-Dissolution

Immediately after the Dissolution, monastic sites were either sold off on the open market or, in some cases, passed on to Henry VIII's supporters as reward for past loyalty. The churches were plundered for valuables and the lead stripped from their roofs, but the fate of the domestic ranges varied from site to site, often depending on their location.

Many of those that were not simply demolished for their materials were converted into dwellings of varying degrees of elegance and grandeur. Some survive today as fine country houses, Forde and Lacock Abbeys being two of the most impressive. Some abbeys and priories were converted on a more modest scale. Only part of the ruins were turned into dwellings, while unused buildings were left to the mercy of the environment; their fate often depended on the quality of the original construction and the harshness of the climate.

Valle Crucis (see p. 132) is a charming example of an abbey that was partially transformed into a private dwelling, taking advantage of the improvements already made to the east range by the abbot for his private apartments. The crudely fashioned fireplace was inserted by the new owners, who used a thirteenth-century gravestone as a 'designer' lintel. Evidence of the abbey's continued use as a farmhouse is provided by the cast iron grate, which is most definitely not sixteenth-century in origin.

FURNESS ABBEY, BARROW-IN-FURNESS, CUMBRIA

Originally a Savignac foundation but amalgamated into the Cistercian order in 1147, Furness was established by Stephen, Count de Blois, some twelve years before he gained the English throne as King Stephen in 1135. When the abbey was surrendered in 1537, it was the second richest Cistercian house in the country; only Fountains had accumulated greater wealth. Furness Abbey's location in a steep-sided natural amphitheatre known as the Vale of Nightshade seems a world away from the nearby shipyards of Barrow, which launched Britain's nuclear submarines for so many years. The site could not be more typically Cistercian: well wooded for timber, close to sources of stone, amply supplied with fresh water – and miles from anywhere. Modern-day travellers to Barrow might agree that it is not the easiest place to get to, so communication links during the Middle Ages must have been almost impossible. To the north are the impassable fells and bogs of southern Lakeland, and to the east the wide expanse of Morecambe Bay, which separates the Barrow peninsula from the 'mainland'. Sections of the bay are passable at low tide, but the temptingly golden sands can be deceptive and many, unfamiliar with the safe routes, have perished in quicksand or drowned when caught by lightning-fast incoming tides. One only has to clamber up the

grassy slope beyond the abbey's southern boundary to get a marvellous view of the red sandstone ruins, their colour muted by age and grey lichen. The south and west ranges have been reduced to ground level, but fortunately most of the east claustral range is intact, endowing the whole site with a sense of scale that makes one appreciate the abbey's status. Nothing exemplifies this more than the stunning row of five decorated arches that grace the east range, the central one being the entrance to the chapter house, which in its complete form must have been outstandingly beautiful. Creative use was made of polished dark marble; this effect was enhanced by the brightness of limewashed walls, a technique employed in many medieval churches. Traces of original Savignac work can be seen around the church, representing a far more decorative style than the austere approach favoured by the 'white monks'. Much of the nave has disappeared, leaving the west tower, transepts and chancel more or less complete. Both chancel and tower were rebuilt during the fifteenth century owing to the collapse of the earlier crossing tower, which unfortunately fell eastwards and demolished that part of the church. In the reconstructed presbytery by the high altar are some of the most perfect sedilia in the country. These stone seats, used by those officiating and assisting at Mass, are crowned by intricately carved canopies.

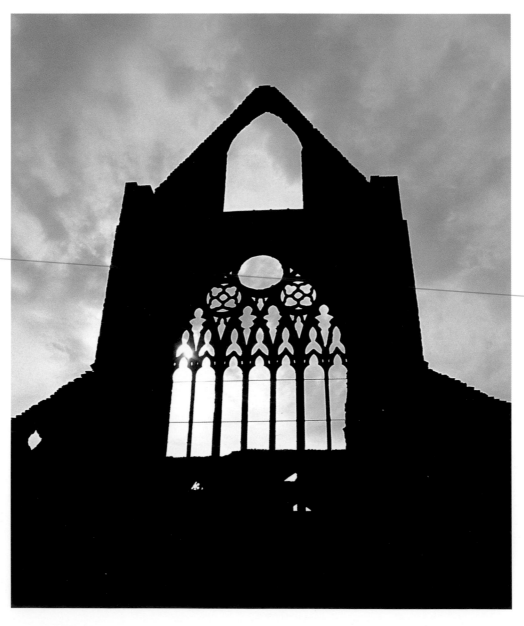

TINTERN ABBEY, NR CHEPSTOW, GWENT, WALES

By far the best time to savour Tintern's mystical atmosphere is on a crisp autumn morning, shortly after sunrise when mist carpets the valley floor, sending tendrils swirling up golden wooded hillsides. At this time the day's first coaches have not yet arrived to disgorge another batch of video-tourists, looking through viewfinders but seeing nothing.

The road through the Wye Valley linking Monmouth and Chepstow maintains an almost parallel course with the river and climbs quite sharply as it heads south from Tintern. From this vantage point one gets a wonderful retrospective view of the monastery, dominated by its hugely impressive late thirteenth-century church. Although built in traditional cruciform shape, the church does not conform with Cistercian simplicity in other respects, and this departure is perfectly highlighted by the west front of the building. Twin doorways are contained within a larger arch adorned with decorative panels, above which the great seven-light west window with fourteenth-century tracery almost intact completes a composition of some considerable style.

It is most surprising to encounter a monastic church in such a full state of preservation, virtually complete apart from the roof. Nevertheless, most of the surrounding domestic and claustral buildings are in the condition one normally expects — severely truncated

having been plundered for stone after the Dissolution. A factor that probably helped preserve the church's fabric was its non-involvement in any major conflicts. The main areas of rebellion against the English throne were centred much further north, leaving Tintern in the peaceful seclusion that the Cistercians sought for all their houses. For reasons of site management and drainage, the claustral buildings were located north of the church and extended down towards the river bank. The number of monks at the abbey probably never exceeded twenty and had fallen to thirteen when the abbey was dissolved in 1536, though even this number was considerably higher than many monasteries could boast of during their last years.

Notwithstanding the ruinous state of many claustral buildings, several interesting reminders of daily monastic routine survive. One such is a canopied recess in the cloister in which a prior would sit and supervise study periods, a scene that one suspects may be not unfamiliar in boarding schools today, although perhaps without the cloistered setting.

Founded in 1131 by Walter fitz Richard, Lord of Chepstow, Tintern is the second oldest Cistercian house in Britain. Although wealthy by Welsh standards, it did not achieve the same financial status as many similar monasteries in England, despite deriving income from granges as far away as Norfolk and farming 3,000 head of sheep.

RIEVAULX ABBEY, NR HELMLSLEY, NORTH YORKSHIRE

Rievaulx's name originates from the River Rye, which flows close to the abbey, whose ruins occupy a secluded site at the end of a deeply wooded valley. Directly overlooking the abbey is Rievaulx Terrace, a half-mile-long promenade of eighteenth-century landscaping by local landowner Thomas Duncombe. He was no doubt inspired by the Romantic movement to create a feature of the magnificent ruins, but, unlike others during that period, he was quite content to admire the view without meddling with its contents. Mature trees now obliterate much of the view down from the Terrace, although occasional teasing glimpses through dense summer foliage become more revealing as leaves succumb to winter's arrival.

The abbey was established in 1132 on land granted by Walter l'Espec, Lord of Helmsley, who had already founded the Augustinian house at Kirkham (see p. 84) nearly a decade before. Rievaulx was first colonized by a group of monks who had travelled over from the French monastery of Clairvaux under the leadership of William, an Englishman who was appointed the community's first abbot.

Work on both church and claustral buildings progressed at great speed during the remaining decades of the twelfth century, and before its close, the abbey's population had risen to somewhere in the region of one

hundred and forty monks supported by around five hundred lay brothers, a phenomenal number that must have presented complex logistical problems in terms of accommodation, catering and hygiene.

Rievaulx's abbot during part of that expansion was St Ailred, a monk whose sanctity, wisdom and literacy substantially enhanced the abbey's reputation as one of the leading monastic communities in the country. That status was retained after his death and certainly contributed to Rievaulx's survival during the lean years that followed towards the end of the fourteenth century. By that time, the population had dwindled to little more than a dozen monks and even fewer lay workers. Although numbers did improve slightly after the Black Death, the abbey never fully recovered from the effects of the plague and the mountain of debts incurred during the earlier ambitious building programme.

Despite its nave being no more than a line of stumpy pier bases, Rievaulx's church remains an imposing structure, a glorious reminder of that period during the early thirteenth century when the English Gothic style came to the fore in religious architecture. That design evolution is clearly illustrated at Rievaulx where rounded, less flamboyant Romanesque windows in parts of the transepts are superseded by the elegant, pointed arches and tiers of smaller openings, which combine so harmoniously in the arcades, triforium and clerestory of the chancel.

BUILDWAS ABBEY,
NR IRONBRIDGE, SHROPSHIRE

Buildwas was established as a daughter house of Furness Abbey (see p. 108) in 1135 by Roger de Clinton, Bishop of Coventry. The abbey was built next to the River Severn, 2 miles upstream from the world's first iron bridge, erected by Abraham Darby in 1778 over 640 years after the monks began work on their equally impressive construction. One of the most remarkable aspects about Buildwas is that it exhibits virtually no changes of architectural style. A contributing factor to such a lack of variation was the abbey's fairly untroubled history, which has left the fabric intact. There were one or two occasions when raiders from Wales caused a few problems, but no serious structural damage resulted. It was perhaps just as well that no major building projects had to be undertaken, as the abbey was not particularly richly endowed. Vital income was derived from collecting tolls on the adjacent river bridge. Buildwas has a feeling of great power, an impression created by the huge piers supporting the nave, the arches of which are good examples of Transitional architecture, that exploratory period when rounded Norman arches started to become more pointed. In contrast, the chapter house is an altogether more subtle place: four slender pillars support a rib-vaulted roof, beneath which a carefully preserved patchwork of medieval floor tiles adds a welcome touch of colour to typically austere surroundings.

CALDER ABBEY,
NR EGREMONT, CUMBRIA

Although Calder Abbey is on private land and not open to the public, the ruins can be appreciated from a public footpath that overlooks the site. The river that gave its name to the abbey only flows a further 3 miles before entering the Irish Sea just below Sellafield amid the far less appealing surroundings of a nuclear processing plant. There has been no attempt at Calder to 'landscape' the site or turn it into a romantic ruin, despite the closeness of the eighteenth-century house created from the south claustral ranges and other buildings. The gradual intrusion of nature endows the ruins with a mysterious atmosphere, as foliage creeps along walls and twists through windows adding greatly to the abbey's appeal. The ruins may be slightly unkempt and overgrown, but those parts of the church that are still standing do so to a good height, especially the tall crossing arches that still carry the base of a tower. Calder's history began in 1135 when it was colonized by monks from Furness Abbey (see p. 108), but their occupation was short-lived because of lack of funds and the unwelcome attention of Scottish raiders. That particular group of monks wandered over to Yorkshire where they ended up founding Byland Abbey (see p. 127) instead. They were replaced in 1142 by another group, who succeeded in sustaining the abbey, although it never achieved prosperity.

FOUNTAINS ABBEY, NR RIPON, NORTH YORKSHIRE

Few would argue with the fact that the majority of people throughout the world are constantly striving to improve their quality of life through better living and working conditions.

Yet one of Britain's greatest medieval monasteries was conceived for exactly the opposite reasons by a group of monks from the Benedictine abbey of St Mary's in York.

Prior Richard and several monks had become disenchanted with their abbey's lax regime, which seemed so removed from St Benedict's original Rule. These feelings were exacerbated when they met some French Cistercians who passed through York on their way to the new foundation at Rievaulx (see p. 112). Their aura of piety and discipline strengthened Richard's resolve, and after much passionate debate he took his supporters to some land near Ripon donated by Archbishop Thurstan of York who sympathized with their ideals. 'Back to basics' is not an entirely new concept dreamed up by twentieth-century politicians, although most would welcome being credited with an original thought!

The manicured landscaping and water gardens of Studley Royal, amid which the abbey ruins are set, bear no resemblance to the sight that would have greeted the monks in the winter of 1132, but the River Skell's wild, overgrown valley perfectly suited their overwhelming desire for peace and isolation.

After a faltering start, Fountains grew to be the wealthiest Cistercian house in Britain, with estates, granges and land as far afield as the Lake District to the west and stretching north up to Teesdale. The Pennines proved ideal land for sheep rearing and vast revenues accrued from the lucrative wool trade. When one considers the ideals that led to Fountains' establishment, it seems quite extraordinary that it should have expanded so rapidly into a large business organization with lavish guest suites for distinguished visitors, basic self-sufficiency becoming a thing of the past.

In common with all Cistercian monasteries, Fountains employed lay brothers to manage the day-to-day running of its agricultural and industrial interests; this workforce probably outnumbered the monks by around four to one by the end of the twelfth century, a period of sustained economic growth and expansion. Much rebuilding took place during the thirteenth century, most notably in the church, where the graceful Early English Chapel of the Nine Altars was a major addition to the east end.

The River Skell's course was skilfully diverted to flow through the very heart of the monastery, thereby ensuring adequate drainage for the large population. Separate infirmaries and latrines for monks and lay brothers were built directly over the stream, which carried debris away from the site. The tranquil waters that now feature in countless photographs of the abbey

would certainly have made a far less appealing foreground during the fourteenth century.

Serious setbacks occurred during the latter decades of the 1300s, when many outlying granges were plundered by Scottish raiders and the Black Death took a heavy toll on the lay brothers. Yet Fountains' resources were sufficient to overcome such problems and a further period of regeneration and building took place under Abbot Huby, architect of the great Perpendicular tower of 1500 that still dominates the ruined abbey.

The church is undoubtedly an outstanding feature, but of all the claustral buildings that have survived so well, the cellarium is by far the most impressive. Its impact is increased by the absence of original partitioning, which provides an uninterrupted view down its entire length of over 300 feet, while its glorious double-aisled, rib-vaulted roof is supported by a line of central columns.

Over half the space was taken up by the lay refectory, then at the centre was the cellarer's parlour, followed by a storage area and finally, nearest the church, the outer parlour. This opened on to the great court and was where monastic business with outsiders was conducted, one of the few places in the monastery where conversation might be heard.

MELROSE ABBEY, MELROSE, BORDERS, SCOTLAND

In common with neighbouring Borders abbeys, Melrose suffered dreadfully as a result of its precariously close proximity to England, being subjected to attacks of varying severity during the cross-border conflicts that punctuated the Middle Ages. Scotland's alliance with France during the fourteenth century led to an attempted invasion of England, which merely served to bring havoc and destruction to the border country when Richard II led an English army north on a retaliatory mission in 1385. In this attack Melrose was almost totally demolished.

The monks had no option but to rebuild their church completely, and most of what is on view today dates from that renaissance. It is difficult to equate such a flamboyant architectural essay in late Decorated and early Perpendicular styles with customary Cistercian austerity, but by the time reconstruction got under way, a more relaxed approach to monastic life had permeated many orders and so the finest stonemasons were employed to create a new church. The surviving ruins are without doubt one of the most magnificent sights in Britain today. Although the life of St Cuthbert is woven into the histories of both Lindisfarne (see p.58) and Durham (see p. 56), it was at Melrose that his vocation began – in the Celtic monastery at Old Melrose, a few miles away from the abbey's present location. Cuthbert was a local shepherd and his

entry into the Church allegedly resulted from a dramatic vision he experienced one night in 651 while out on the fells with his sheep, in which he saw a great light surrounded by angels bearing a soul up towards heaven. This vision coincided with St Aidan's death, and Cuthbert thereafter pledged to continue the work of spreading the Gospel throughout Northumbria.

The Cistercian foundation at Melrose dates back to 1136 when one of the great early reformers of the Scottish church, King David I, invited monks from Rievaulx (see p. 112) to establish a monastery at Melrose. The site that existed there proved unsuitable and so building began where Melrose stands today, but only small fragments of any twelfth-century work survive.

Both transepts and presbytery are remarkable for their ornamentation, not just in the fine, flowing tracery of the windows but also the gargoyles, sculptures and other carved details that adorn the exterior walls. Binoculars are an invaluable aid in studying those details beyond the reach of the naked eye, such as humorous figures, grotesque mythical creatures and, high up in the apex of the east gable, an exquisite portrayal of the Coronation of the Virgin.

Three bays of the redundant nave were used to form a parish church, in use until 1810, but unfortunately its functional roof has been left in place, a drab intrusion into otherwise glorious surroundings.

JERVAULX ABBEY, NR LEYBURN, NORTH YORKSHIRE

Jervaulx Abbey may be privately owned but it is always open to the public, an 'honesty box' by the entrance gate replacing the visitor centres and site museums usually associated with leading monastic sites. Although obviously cared for and maintained to a degree, the ruins remain delightfully unkempt, and in early summer, walls, pillars and arches are festooned by colourful wild flowers that sprout from every nook and cranny.

'Jervaulx' is a French interpretation of Wensleydale's original name of Yorevale, derived from the River Ure that flows through the dale. The monks who eventually settled here in 1156 had originally established a community some 15 miles further west near Aysgarth. They had abandoned that site after nine years of struggling to exist surrounded by totally unproductive land, an insurmountable problem for Cistercians, who were renowned for generating much of their wealth from sheep farming and wool exports. The abbey's setting could not be more appealing, as one has to approach on foot across wooded parkland. One of the first exhibits encountered is a large stone trough, which, although it resembles a cattle trough, was actually the vessel in which abbots were embalmed after death, Several of them were laid to rest beneath the chapter house.

Of the church, there are scant remains as it was completely destroyed on the

orders of Henry VIII after Jervaulx's last abbot, Adam Sedbar, had been implicated in the 'Pilgrimage of Grace', a northern-based rebellion against the Dissolution. This false accusation led to his imprisonment in the Tower of London and subsequent execution. Many monastic churches were merely stripped of their roof lead and left to the mercy of the elements, but those that were deemed to be in any way involved in the revolt against suppression were razed to the ground to prevent reoccupation by defiant monks. Other buildings have fared better, and the most notable surviving example is the almost complete west wall of the monks' dormitory, which was 173 feet long. Its upper-storey lancet windows are still in place. Sockets in the stonework alongside the windows probably housed sections of timber used to form individual cubicles.

In its customary location to the east of the cloister, the chapter house is entered down a flight of six steps, still framed on either side by round arched windows, and traces of the entrance portal have been left standing. Fortunately, several of the original pillars used to support a vaulted roof are still in place, and their finely decorated capitals provide a touch of finesse amid so much fragmented masonry.

ROCHE ABBEY, NR MALTBY, SOUTH YORKSHIRE

Roche Abbey was the first of several medieval monasteries to receive the attentions of eighteenth-century landscape designer Lancelot 'Capability' Brown, during a period when such ruins were regarded as decorative features rather than important archaeological and historical sites. The Fourth Earl of Scarborough commissioned Brown to reorganize the grounds of the family seat at Sandbeck Park, his contract stipulating that the work should be carried out with 'poet's feeling and painter's eye'.

Brown's interpretation of that brief resulted in the demolition of surviving claustral buildings and other parts of the site, and what remained above ground was obliterated by tons of earth to form extensive terracing. A vast area of parkland was then appropriately planted, and streams and watercourses were harnessed into waterfalls and an ornamental lake, leaving the abbey church's transepts as the only visible feature.

In mitigation, by the time Brown was consulted, there may already have been fewer buildings left standing than one might have expected from such an imposing, stone-built complex. A contemporary account of the abbey's fate immediately following Roche's surrender at the Dissolution describes a frenzy of looting and destruction by local townsfolk, possibly motivated as much by resentment of Cistercian affluence as by pure greed.

The site has now been meticulously excavated to reveal every detail of its original layout, and although its walls are only a foot or so high, one's pleasure in exploring the ruins is scarcely diminished. A bone-crunching cobbled lane bordered on either side by dense foliage winds down to the valley floor, whose northern edge is dominated by a dramatic, white limestone cliff.

Roche was founded in 1147 and that part of the church that has survived can be dated to the late twelfth century. The pointed arches of the transepts represent one of the earliest examples of the Gothic style in the north of England, although the clerestory windows above appear more rounded, following more traditional Norman architecture.

Maltby Beck flows through the site, at one point crossed by an elegant arched bridge built when the refectory was extended southwards. The stream is spanned by other buildings further along the site, and the last in line, unsurprisingly, are the latrines.

Away from the heart of the monastic complex, the great abbey gatehouse has survived remarkably intact, with its different sized gates designed for carriages and pedestrians still in place beneath vaulted portals.

Although havoc ensued after the monks left, the ceremony of surrender was conducted with dignity and the abbot and eighteen monks were generously rewarded not only with pensions but also a 'demob' clothing allowance.

ABBEY DORE, GOLDEN VALLEY, HEREFORDSHIRE

Few other parts of the English countryside could be so enchantingly named as Herefordshire's Golden Valley, although an explanation for the valley's name and that of the Cistercian abbey founded here in 1147 by Robert FitzHarold probably has more to do with linguistics than actual colour. The Welsh referred to the valley's river as 'dwr', meaning 'water' – a word sounding exactly like the French phrase for 'golden', 'd'or'. So perhaps the Normans who built the abbey simply misunderstood and thought the river was called Golden, and therefore so was the valley. In that case, they may have decided, they had better build a golden abbey, hence Abbey Dore! Colour is very much a feature of the abbey – the dark red sandstone of its exterior and the kaleidoscope of light that floods in through refined lancet windows to brighten the lofty interior, maybe even to play across the chain mail, sword and shield of the founder's full size stone effigy. Very few monastic churches saved for parish worship made use of the eastern end, but Abbey Dore is one of the exceptions, retaining the presbytery, crossing and transepts. The church is an outstanding example of Early English architecture, its restrained beauty somehow accentuated by the later Jacobean fittings introduced by Viscount Scudamore during a seventeenth-century restoration that included the use of over 200 tons of oak for a new roof.

BYLAND ABBEY, NR COXWOLD, NORTH YORKSHIRE

Byland Abbey's church may be little more than a three-sided empty shell, but the survival of its west end has endowed Byland with one of the most stunning monastic landmarks in the country. The great rose window that once adorned the nave's entrance was 26 feet in diameter and must have been an awe-inspiring sight when the church was in daily use. Directly below the window, three large, slender lancets create a perfectly balanced composition, whose drama is doubly enhanced when thrown into silhouette by sunset's palette of red and gold.

Those monks who built Byland had endured many tribulations prior to establishing one of the north's great Cistercian houses, which ranked almost as highly as its illustrious near neighbours Fountains (see p. 116) and Rievaulx (see p. 112). Abbot Gerold and a group of monks had made the long journey from Cumbria to Yorkshire following a dispute with their own house at Furness (see p. 108). They first established an abbey at Calder (see p. 115) from which they were forced to retreat after savage attacks by Scottish raiders; they were subsequently refused entry back into Furness and travelled across England to enlist support from the Archbishop of York.

The wandering monks were eventually granted land by their new patron, Roger de Mowbray, some two miles east of Rievaulx at a place now occupied only

by the tiny village of Old Byland. But the monks' tenure there was also short-lived because of a squabble with their Cistercian neighbours over church bells. Extraordinary as it may seem, the ringing from one monastery carried across to the other and vice versa, causing such inconvenience to both parties that the only answer to the impasse was the departure of one community.

The Byland monks and their offending bells moved further south to a temporary location near Coxwold, eventually settling for the last time in 1177 on a low-lying site that required extensive drainage work to make it viable. Once they had finally established a permanent home, building work progressed rapidly to produce one of the finest abbey churches completed during the early thirteenth century. Two design features particular to Byland are the carved waterleaf mouldings that appear on many capitals and the green and yellow floor tiles used throughout, some of which remain in place around the south transept and crossing. The best examples have been preserved and transferred to the site museum, but those that do survive *in situ* show how gloriously colourful the 330-foot-long church must have once appeared.

The museum also houses other valuable artefacts and fragments of masonry overlooked or discarded by those who plundered the site for materials when the abbey was abandoned. One of the most surprising and poignant finds

unearthed during early twentieth-century excavations was a large stone inkwell, thought to be from the chapter house and likely to have been used by those parties involved in signing Byland over to Henry VIII's Commissioners when the abbey was surrendered in November 1538.

Few of the claustral buildings have survived to any great height, but the precise layout of everything can be easily traced. One notable departure from the norm was a narrow thoroughfare running alongside the lay brothers' accommodation. The lay brothers were responsible for most of the manual work, enabling the choir monks to concentrate solely on their spiritual activities. They were usually housed in a monastery's west range, but at Byland it seems they were provided with what amounted to their own cloister, complete with recessed seating in one wall.

Not all the abbey's precinct is clearly defined, although some idea of its original scale can be gleaned from the presence of a gatehouse arch some distance away from the church and now incorporated into farm buildings. Anyone wishing to visit the nearby village of Oldfield by anything larger than a conventional motor car would be well advised to find an alternative route, as the medieval stone archway that straddles the public highway certainly did not anticipate the demands of twentieth-century traffic.

VALLE CRUCIS ABBEY, NR LLANGOLLEN, DENBIGHSHIRE, WALES

The road heading north from Llangollen towards the Horseshoe Pass climbs up through the Valley of the Cross (Valle Crucis), after which the Cistercian abbey is named. The cross is the Pillar of Eliseg, an ancestral memorial erected by Cyngen, the ninth-century king of Powys, and a sizeable fragment of it still stands not far from the abbey.

Surrounded by dramatic scenery, the ruins have attracted many artists over the centuries, particularly towards the end of the eighteenth century when the abbey was portrayed in post-Dissolution mode, a farmhouse amid romantic ruins. Although the landscape has changed little since then, that setting of pastoral tranquillity has been shattered by the presence of an ugly caravan park immediately next to the ruined church.

Founded in 1201, Valle Crucis was probably never occupied by more than the thirteen monks who colonized it initially, and by the sixteenth century their number had dwindled to a mere handful. Much of the western ranges are now no more than foundations, but parts of the church and eastern claustral buildings survive almost to full height, particularly those that formed the later dwelling.

Much of the church dates from the thirteenth century, and the most impressive part is the west front whose impact is increased by the diminished

nave walls on either side. The gable end with a rose window was replaced midway through the fourteenth century; the addition is clearly marked by the use of stone blocks substantially larger than the materials used for the lower courses. Of the rest of the church, both the south transept and the east end survive, but undoubtedly the greatest interest lies within the east range, containing the chapter house and the first-floor monks' dormitory. The chapter house is in excellent condition, probably built early in the fifteenth century. It has a most harmonious interior, an effect enhanced by the absence of capitals on the pillars, thus creating an uninterrupted, graceful, flowing movement from floor level up into the vaulted roof.

A narrow flight of steps next to the chapter house leads up to the dormitory and abbot's chamber, and it is these rooms that formed the basis of the later conversion. It appears that towards the end of the fifteenth century, the abbot had adopted a lifestyle alien to Cistercian rules and forced the remaining monks to sleep elsewhere when he created comfortable guest apartments from the southern part of the dormitory. Visitors to Valle Crucis were apparently moved to comment on the unexpected quality of hospitality provided by the abbot of an order noted for its strict behavioural guidelines, but perhaps this was merely symptomatic of universally sliding standards within the monastic community.

SWEETHEART ABBEY, NEW ABBEY, DUMFRIES AND GALLOWAY, SCOTLAND

Even if Sweetheart Abbey were little more than a shapeless mound of rubble, it would still merit inclusion in this book for its name alone, but as a striking red sandstone building of some character, it justifies its place for its appearance, too. The manner in which the last Cistercian monastery established in Britain acquired its title could be regarded either as sentimentally touching or simply macabre and more suited to Mary Shelley's Gothic tale about a creature made of human body parts.

Lady Devorgilla of Galloway and her husband, John Balliol, were so deeply devoted to each other that, following Balliol's death in 1269, his grieving widow sought more than memories by which to remember him. She had his heart removed and embalmed, then placed it in an ivory casket that never left her side; she referred to this most precious possession as her 'sweet, silent companion'. Her action was probably no more bizarre than churches accumulating miscellaneous digits to display as saintly relics.

Four years after her bereavement, Lady Devorgilla founded the Cistercian monastery as a lasting memorial to her husband, and upon her own death twenty years after her partner, she was buried in the abbey church clutching the ivory casket. The monks were so moved by her enduring love that it was decided the abbey should be named in her

honour and was thereafter known in Latin as 'Dulce Cor', or 'Sweetheart'. The abbey was not the sole beneficiary of Devorgilla's generosity, as she had established or was patron of several other friaries and chaplaincies in the region, and, in addition, pledged her continued patronage and support to the Oxford college founded by her husband – Balliol College is one of the university's three oldest academic foundations.

Another John Balliol, Devorgilla's son, also features in history books, but as a short-lived and somewhat ineffectual vassal king of Scotland, appointed by Edward I following a disputed succession. Scotland's later alliance with France resulted in Edward storming north to crush the Scots army at Dunbar. He accepted the submission of Scotland's great men and the abdication of John Balliol, and even seized the Stone of Destiny from Scone Castle during a whirlwind campaign in which his contemptuous treatment of the Scots led to many years of fighting and the emergence of folk heroes such as Robert Bruce and William Wallace. Sweetheart does not appear to have suffered excessive material damage during the wars with England, despite Edward I's army being encamped nearby for a week in 1300. The greatest threat to the abbey's survival was sheer neglect caused by lack of funds, as the Balliol estates and other resources had been forfeited to the English crown, leaving the monastic community without patronage.

A saviour was found in Archibald Douglas, Lord of Galloway, who had been persuaded by King David II to give financial support to the floundering monastery, which by the end of the fourteenth century was in a state of some disrepair. Archibald was known by two nicknames, either 'Black' or 'Grim', both earned for his conduct during battles with the English. So the 'white' monks found themselves a new benefactor in 'Black' Archibald, who formally signed the deeds of patronage in 1381. Additional income was derived four years later when a chantry was established for several members of the Douglas family. This was a common medieval practice whereby the wealthy paid for prayers to be regularly offered up on their behalf.

That the church has survived almost intact is largely thanks to a group of public-spirited local people who actively sought to preserve it towards the end of the eighteenth century, preventing further plundering of the site for stone. Almost every trace of monastic building has disappeared and the stated ideals of those who saved the abbey church 'as an ornament to this part of the country' certainly hold good today. The roofless red sandstone building provides a picturesque background to the low, whitewashed cottages lining New Abbey's main street. The village became known by that name to avoid confusion between Sweetheart and Dundrennan Abbeys, the latter being older and located slightly further west.

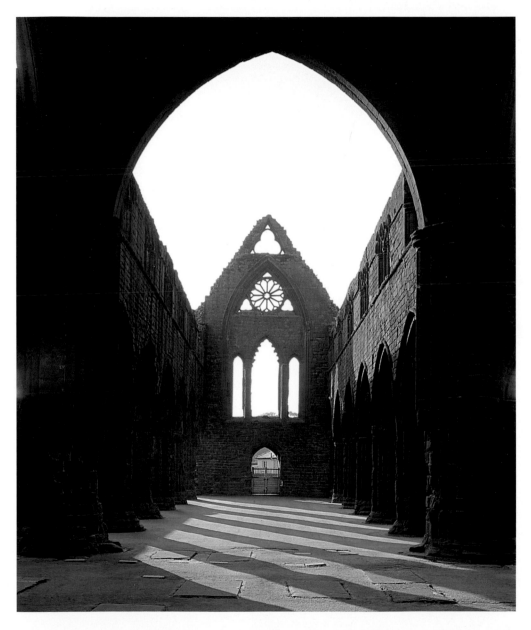

Lady Devorgilla's monument is housed in the south transept and unsurprisingly depicts her clasping a heart to her bosom. This sculpture was reconstructed from fragments unearthed during twentieth-century restorations. Both ends of the church feature equally dramatic windows: the west end was remodelled from its original large single format into three lights topped by a rose window, and the two sections are separated by an additional band of masonry to provide greater strength to that gable end. Most claustral buildings may have disappeared, but one outstanding legacy of Sweetheart's monastic history has survived in a substantial portion of the precinct wall that originally encompassed the entire site of 30 acres. Fashioned from huge granite blocks, the wall often exceeds 8 feet and erecting it must have been a monumental task, not to mention the work involved in constructing the buildings themselves.

Premonstratensians, Cluniacs and Carthusians

Shap Abbey
(Premonstratensian),
Nr Shap, Cumbria

The Premonstratensian penchant for establishing monasteries in isolated locations was taken to extremes when the order accepted the gift of land at Shap from Thomas fitz Gospatrick. If criteria for the choice of site included being one of the wettest and most inhospitable landscapes in England, with an almost impossible journey to the nearest shops, Shap was an ideal candidate. The abbey's remoteness did have one distinct advantage, however – it enabled the abbey to survive the Dissolution until 1540, four years longer than many of its contemporaries, and one might imagine the Commissioners drawing lots to decide who would make the arduous journey to carry out Henry VIII's order. When the abbey was finally dissolved and the canons dispersed, the last abbot received an exceedingly generous pension of £40 a year. Shap was founded at the end of the twelfth century, and although never a large house it was quite well endowed, holding substantial tracts of land in surrounding parishes. The site is almost on the banks of the River Lowther and, despite the surrounding open spaces, is fairly cramped in a small hollow. Most of the ruins are but a couple of feet high, an exception being the late fifteenth-century tower, whose survival provides the site with an important visual balance. A large farmhouse beyond the precinct wall was obviously constructed using stone from the redundant buildings.

The Premonstratensians were a reforming order under Augustinian rule, motivated by the same intense ideals that had earlier resulted in the creation of the Cistercians. The order was named after the remote forest hamlet of Premontre, near Laon in north-eastern France, where St Norbert had retreated following several failed attempts to persuade existing communities of canons to follow a more vigorously religious life.

Norbert eventually attracted a band of disciples to his isolated base, and the new movement was finally established in 1121. Its members were referred to as the 'white canons', for they elected to wear habits of the same colour as their Cistercian role models. Similarities were not restricted to apparel, as the Premonstratensians structured their order in the same manner as Cîteaux with regard to the authority and control exercised by the mother house.

The Cluniacs originate from the monastery of Cluny in Burgundy. The order became renowned for its almost obsessive form of worship, which placed great emphasis on elaborate ritual and ceremony in surroundings of grandeur. So much time was devoted to cycles of prayer and worship that Cluniacs engaged in almost no manual labour and very little study.

Visitors to the abbey at Cluny were frequently overwhelmed by the sumptuous hospitality provided by the abbot, in contrast to more customary monastic fare. Allegedly, the explanation for such high standards of cuisine was that the demands made upon the body by such rigorous and constant worship required an appropriately substantial diet.

The Cluniacs became a major force in English monasticism, but, although a total of over thirty houses existed at the time of the Dissolution, the order's complete allegiance to the French mother house had limited appeal to potential patrons.

The Carthusians, by far the most austere of all monastic orders, sought a return to the extreme monasticism associated with early Christian monks who lived as hermits in the Egyptian desert. English Carthusian houses were known as Charterhouses, a name derived from the order's first monastery at La Grande Chartreuse near Grenoble.

Only nine houses were established in England, the first of which was Witham Priory in Somerset towards the end of the twelfth century. The movement obviously had its devotees, but the degree of privation demanded of Carthusians must have restricted recruitment to an order that referred to its members as 'Christ's Poor Men'.

MUCH WENLOCK PRIORY (CLUNIAC), MUCH WENLOCK, SHROPSHIRE

Much Wenlock lies at the northern end of Wenlock Edge, a limestone escarpment providing unparalleled views across the Shropshire countryside. This landscape is celebrated in the poetry of A. E. Housman, particularly in 'A Shropshire Lad'. The small market town that initially grew up around the Cluniac priory has remained pleasantly untouched by unsympathetic modern expansion. Narrow streets run through its medieval core linking Guildhall, town gaol, market hall and parish church, behind which a lane leads down to the priory of St Milburga. The priory has always retained the name of its original founder, a daughter of the seventh-century King Merewald of Mercia. Towards the end of the ninth century, the Scandinavian hand of destruction mercilessly extended to this rural retreat, leaving Milburga's nunnery in ruins. In the years immediately preceding the Norman Conquest, another foundation was established on the site by Leofric, husband of Lady Godiva, and although evidence of that church has been uncovered, the ruins visible today are from the monastery endowed by one of William I's staunchest supporters, Roger Montgomery, created Earl of Shrewsbury in 1070. Having been a generous benefactor of the abbey at Cluny in Burgundy, Montgomery decided that Much Wenlock should be a Cluniac house; accordingly, monks

travelled to England from the French priory of La Charité-sur-Loire. As the monastery flourished, increased wealth was ploughed into a rebuilding programme instigated during the thirteenth century to enlarge the church, which in its final form was some 350 feet long. One only has to study the surviving section of the south transept, which stands to almost full height, to appreciate what an impressive structure it must have been, in keeping with the Cluniac ethos of glorifying God through elaborate ritual in magnificent surroundings. One of the priory's outstanding details is the interlaced blind arcading in the Norman chapter house, fortunately retained when the church was rebuilt. Although now roofless, the room originally comprised three vaulted bays, and traces of the supporting pillars and capitals form part of the north wall where the most prolific section of arcading is located. The cloisters also house a remnant from the twelfth century, an unusually ornate octagonal lavatorium located in the south-west corner, immediately in front of the refectory so that monks might wash before entering the dining room. Also around the cloisters, but definitely not medieval, are yew bushes perfectly clipped to represent an assortment of birds and animals. A sumptuous dwelling was fashioned from the prior's lodgings and adjoining infirmary, but it has been in constant private ownership since the Dissolution and no longer forms part of the monastic site.

CASTLE ACRE PRIORY (CLUNIAC), CASTLE ACRE, NORFOLK

William de Warenne, Second Earl of Surrey and William the Conqueror's son-in-law, built the huge motte and bailey castle from which Castle Acre village derives its name. When he founded the priory in 1089, he was maintaining the family tradition of supporting the Cluniac order from Burgundy – his father had been responsible for establishing the order's first monastery on English soil at Lewes in East Sussex. The priory stands alone in fields near the River Nar, its outline made more distinct by the white stone and flint used for construction. When work got under way, de Warenne further assisted the monks by providing them with the services of his own stonemason. Whether this man's craftsmanship contributed to any buildings on the current site is unclear as the monastery originally began life closer to the village within the castle's outer defences, a location that proved unworkable. Two of the most complete surviving parts of the priory could arguably symbolize the rise and fall of monasticism in this country. The church's west front exhibits some of the finest Norman architectural decoration anywhere in England, a striking testimony to those who laboured for love. Standing at right angles adjoining the church is the prior's lodging, which bears closer resemblance to a secular medieval manor house than a monastic dwelling, a clear indication of the style

and grandeur that some abbots and priors deemed appropriate to their rank. Small wonder that Henry VIII eventually moved against the monasteries when such implied wealth, often tinged with decadence, was being so openly flaunted in some institutions during the fifteenth and early sixteenth centuries. Castle Acre's income and material possessions were severely taxed by the English monarchs Edward I, Edward II and Edward III during the numerous wars and quarrels with France that persisted during the Middle Ages. Its direct links to the mother house in Cluny endowed Castle Acre and similar monasteries with alien status, a stigma finally removed after naturalization was granted in 1351, albeit on payment of a fairly substantial 'facility fee'. It is remarkable that the stunning array of arcading and other decoration on the west front has survived when so much of the church is in a rather crumbled state, although another notable exception is the south-west tower, whose windows clearly show the progression from rounded Norman to more pointed Early English style. Away from the church, the claustral buildings vary in size and degree of preservation, one of the largest and most complete also being one of the most essential – the reredorter, or monks' latrine. Provision of fresh water and safe sewage disposal were necessary parts of monastic planning, the whole aspect of which is well illustrated at Castle Acre.

DRYBURGH ABBEY (PREMONSTRATENSIAN), NR ST BOSWELLS, BORDERS, SCOTLAND

The three great Borders abbeys of Jedburgh (see p. 90), Melrose (see p. 120) and Dryburgh, all representing different monastic orders, lie within just a few miles of each other in the rolling countryside drained by the Tweed. Dryburgh itself occupies a delightful location within a deep horseshoe loop of this river.

Hugh de Moreville was responsible for the foundation of Dryburgh in 1150, the first Premonstratensian house in Scotland and, during its life, the most important. King David I of Scotland had become friendly with de Moreville during his time in England and it was at his personal invitation that the wealthy landowner travelled north. This move ultimately resulted in his being accorded the powerful title of Constable of Scotland.

For whatever reason, the benefactor decided to enter the abbey himself as a novice some time later, and spent his last years in the midst of the foundation he had created, which would continue to be financed from revenues derived from his original gifts of land. Had de Moreville entered the priory in 1170, one could have well understood his need for solitude, but he died at Dryburgh in 1162, therefore ignorant of his son's implication in the murder of Thomas à Becket, Archbishop of Canterbury, eight years later. Throughout the Middle Ages, Dryburgh was subjected to several

brutal and damaging attacks by English forces, at least two of which almost signalled the end of the abbey. Legend attributes one raid in 1322 to the premature ringing of the abbey's bells in celebration of yet another Scottish victory. Gloating peals echoed across the countryside but, unfortunately for Dryburgh, the defeated English soldiers were still within hearing range and had enough energy to detour from their dispirited march home to teach the canons a lesson.

King Robert the Bruce and other leading figures contributed towards a rebuilding programme, but an even more severe raid in 1385 caused far greater devastation, and much of the church's west end had to be completely rebuilt. The splendid fifteenth-century doorway is now all that survives from that reconstruction, the nave having entirely disappeared. Of the original church, only the thirteenth-century transepts remain; the northern one is the most complete and offers a clear indication of how magnificent the whole building must have been when in use.

Two chapels within the north transept contain the graves of two famous men associated with the Dryburgh area. One was a writer renowned for novels that often featured rugged, swashbuckling characters, while the other was a military commander who had not fantasy heroes at his disposal, but ordinary men, many of whom died performing acts of bravery beyond the imagination of any novelist.

Sir Walter Scott of Abbotsford was buried in 1832, followed under a century later by Field Marshal Earl Haig of Bemersyde in 1928. In death they make an intriguing combination and one might speculate how they would have regarded each other in life. Scott built a mansion at nearby Abbotsford and his name is given to a spectacular viewpoint above the abbey, known as 'Scott's View'. It is alleged that he visited this spot so many times that the horse drawing his hearse to Dryburgh paused there automatically. Earl Haig was a descendant of the La Hague family whose ancestral home had been at Bemersyde, where they had settled after leaving France to serve the abbey's founder, Hugh de Moreville. It is therefore perfectly appropriate that Haig was not only honoured with that title after the Great War, but that his grave should be at Dryburgh.

Despite the damage inflicted on much of the abbey, some of the claustral buildings are in their original form; the most impressive are in the east range. Because the stone is of such fine texture, brightly coloured and untainted in any way by atmospheric pollution, it is hard not to assume that the deeply recessed and ornately carved chapter house and processional doorways are simply modern replicas, installed only a couple of decades ago.

After the church, the chapter house was the most important building in the abbey, and its status is reflected in the grandeur of its entrance door, flanked on either side by fine, twelfth-century

twin-light windows. The interior has a simple barrel-vaulted roof and stone benching round the walls, on which the canons sat during meetings. Immediately to the south, the warming room offered the canons an occasional opportunity to savour the comforts of an open fire before returning to their tasks and devotions in unheated buildings and raw Borders weather. Dryburgh's visual appeal is enhanced by its construction on three levels, rising up from the sixteenth-century gatehouse at the site's southern end. The abbey's natural beauty was not lost on the Eleventh Earl of Buchan, David Steuart Erskine, who purchased it towards the end of the eighteenth century and transformed the cloister into a heavily planted decorative garden, complete with a statue of the architect Inigo Jones. The cloister is now back to neatly mown grass, which is deeply shadowed in late afternoon by the refectory's tall gable end. This solid black shape is broken only by sunlight piercing an elegant rose window, creating a motif on the grass that resembles an ancient Celtic cross.

EASBY ABBEY (PREMONSTRATENSIAN), NR RICHMOND, NORTH YORKSHIRE

Richmond Castle's impregnable Norman keep is clearly visible from the narrow lane that plunges steeply down to the ruins of Easby Abbey, huddled on a cramped, level site by the River Swale. The house for Premonstratensian canons was founded in 1151 by Roal, Constable of Richmond, and although it was not excluded from the attentions of Scottish raiders during the Middle Ages, it was the 'home side' that inflicted most damage when English troops were billeted at Easby prior to the Battle of Neville's Cross in 1346. The most complete and impressive building, surviving to nearly full height, is the monks' frater or dining room on the southern edge of the site. The quality and quantity of the frater's windows could almost mislead one into thinking it was the abbey church, but of that little remains. Because space was at a premium, the builders had to deviate from accepted monastic layout, and placed the church in the centre of the complex instead of to the north, while for reasons of drainage, the monks' dormitory was west of the cloister instead of in its customary position to the east. Another diversion from the norm at Easby is that the thirteenth-century parish church is located within the abbey precincts; the canons provided one of their number to double as priest in charge.

BLANCHLAND ABBEY (PREMONSTRATENSIAN), BLANCHLAND, NORTHUMBERLAND

Premonstratensian canons founded Blanchland Abbey in 1165, segments of which have been incorporated into current buildings. Blanchland is a real curiosity, a model village set among the wild moors and tumbling becks of the Upper Derwent Valley, with stone cottages bordering an immaculately neat square from which cars are banned. The silence can be almost unnerving as one passes into the cloister-like square through the fifteenth-century abbey gatehouse, which now forms the village entrance. This area was once rich in lead and the village was built during the mid-eighteenth century to house workers from the surrounding Lord Crewe mines. This complex derived its name from the Bishop of Durham, Lord Crewe, into whose ownership the monastic estates had passed. The abbey's chancel, north transept and tower survived to form the only Premonstratensian parish church in the country, and of the other buildings, the most notable survivors are the abbot's lodging, the guesthouse and the monastic kitchen, all now part of the village hotel, the Lord Crewe Arms. The original abbot's lodging was built in the form of a fortified pele tower, as Blanchland's exposed position made it vulnerable to attack from the bands of Scottish raiders who plagued the north during the Middle Ages.

COCKERSAND ABBEY (PREMONSTRATENSIAN), NR COCKERMOUTH, LANCASHIRE

Cockersand Abbey must be one of the most intriguing monastic fragments in England. Virtually isolated on the Lune estuary's remote southern shore, its sole companions are a farmhouse, a small offshore lighthouse and the cattle that graze around scattered fragments of half-buried medieval masonry. A priory was established on this site some ten years after it was first occupied in 1180 by a hermit named Hugh Garth. The Premonstratensian community prospered and was promoted to abbatial status and endowed with land across much of Lancashire. The only part of the priory to have survived is the hexagonal chapter house, largely thanks to the Daltons of Thurnham Hall who, having acquired the abbey midway through the sixteenth century, used it as a family mausoleum. Stone from the ruined abbey has been used to strengthen coastal defences, probably saving the chapter house from encroaching coastal erosion. On tranquil summer evenings when advancing high tides sidle silently in across sunset-tinged mudflats one can empathize with the Premonstratensians' desire for absolute solitude. But as winter approaches, storms batter the vulnerable, low-lying coast. On such days one has to acknowledge that to seek out such a place in which to establish a community was in itself an act of faith.

EGGLESTONE ABBEY (PREMONSTRATENSIAN), NR BARNARD CASTLE, COUNTY DURHAM

Founded for Premonstratensian canons towards the end of the twelfth century, Egglestone was often considered too poorly endowed to retain its status as an abbey, but it somehow managed to stave off demotion to a priory. The ruins occupy a dramatic site, perched almost directly above Thorsgill Beck, a tributary of the River Tees, whose peat-stained waters bully their way through a rocky gorge, spanned by Abbey Bridge, in a foaming brown torrent. A road crosses the bridge and climbs to a vantage point that provides not only an impressive view of the abbey in its landscape setting, but also the somewhat incongruous sight of a Renaissance-style French château towering over the ancient market town of Barnard Castle, less than a mile to the north. Built around 1869 by Sir John Bowes, a local magnate, the house is now the Bowes Museum and is renowned for the scope and quality of its collections. The church itself is the major surviving element of the abbey and now contains the elaborately carved tomb of another member of the Bowes family, Sir Ralph. Egglestone's meagre ruins may not boast exhibits to match those housed in the nearby museum, but the delicate, twin lancet, Early English windows that survive in the chancel might be considered the equal of any Old Master.

BAYHAM ABBEY (PREMONSTRATENSIAN), NR TUNBRIDGE WELLS, EAST SUSSEX

Set in the broad, wooded valley of the River Teise, Bayham's ruins literally straddle the Kent/Sussex border, the abbey originally having a gatehouse in both counties. Access to the abbey is past a Gothic villa built by Viscount Camden around 1750, and if first impressions are of incredible neatness, of a garden featuring an elaborate ornamental rockery, one would not be far from the truth. Bayham is one of several abbeys and priories for which the term 'landscaping', as used by certain architects and garden designers during the eighteenth century, was occasionally a euphemism for demolition, although, fortunately in this case, not too much has been levelled in pursuit of an aesthetically pleasing vista. As the Picturesque movement gained momentum, impressionable landowners whose estates encompassed monastic sites sought to transform them from unappealing blots on the landscape into desirable features. Perhaps the prospect of owning such a romantic medieval ruin was viewed as something of a status symbol, at a time when even the most lavish follies could be commissioned with ease. To have a monastery in the garden would certainly have represented a touch of one-upmanship among one's peers. As one of the most fashionable practitioners of this art during the late eighteenth and early nineteenth centuries, Humphrey

Repton was consulted several times by Lord Camden on Bayham's layout, although it would appear that some of his more radical suggestions were only partially implemented. One of his schemes was for the removal of the villa in favour of a grand, castellated building on the far side of the valley. Happily, the villa was retained, serving as the local residence of the Camden family until 1872, at which time they moved to the Victorian mansion that now dominates the skyline to the west. The original abbey church was substantially altered towards the end of the thirteenth century and it is the transepts and crossing piers from that period, standing almost full height, that provide the most impressive remains. Additional remodelling took place during the fifteenth century, evidence of which can be traced in the three tall Perpendicular arches that were inserted into the south wall, supported by buttresses so thick that the cloister walk had to be cut through them in a series of arches. However, of all Bayham's features, the most delightful and idiosyncratic is the giant beech tree that now occupies the site of the original east window, directly behind the high altar. Thick roots twist down from the trunk to disappear among the surviving masonry of the original church wall.

TITCHFIELD ABBEY (PREMONSTRATENSIAN), NR FAREHAM, HAMPSHIRE

Sir Thomas Wriothesley was granted the thirteenth-century Titchfield Abbey in 1537 by Henry VIII's Commissioners and swiftly converted it into a sumptuous Tudor mansion renamed Place House. The work was completed in only five years at the seemingly modest cost of some £200. Of the original abbey, founded in 1232 by Peter des Roches, Bishop of Winchester, little remains above ground, and much of the house was also demolished in the eighteenth century by its new owners to provide building materials for another of their residences. The imposing gatehouse, which has survived nearly intact, was fashioned from the church's nave, although one would be hard-pressed to associate the turrets and crenellations with a house of prayer. In addition to the gatehouse, a more tangible memorial to the Wriothesley family can be found in the nearby parish church in the form of an impressively sculpted alabaster tomb.

Although Titchfield is now 2 miles from the coast, centuries ago the River Meon was navigable as far as the village and so, being not far from Winchester, the abbey made a useful base from which to maintain links with France.

MOUNT GRACE PRIORY (CARTHUSIAN), NR NORTHALLERTON, NORTH YORKSHIRE

One of only ten Charterhouses in England, Mount Grace Priory was founded in 1398 by Richard II's nephew, Thomas de Holand, Earl of Kent and Duke of Surrey, although his personal involvement was peremptorily curtailed by the removal of his head for treason against his uncle's successor, Henry IV, just two years later. Access to the ruins of Mount Grace is through the front door of a seventeenth-century mansion, which was converted from the priory guesthouse and extended again in 1900 into an elegant country house dedicated to the Arts and Crafts movement. Such an entrance into a supposedly humble religious house may come as something of a surprise, but two more surprises await in the priory itself. Compared to the churches of other monastic orders who built on a grand scale, the diminutive place of worship erected by the Carthusians at Mount Grace would not seem incongruous beside a small village green. Yet in complete contrast, the cloister is a huge grassy square large enough to stage a sporting fixture. (What a wonderful image that conjures up — two teams of monks wearing contrasting coloured habits hitched up above the knees, scampering ruddy-faced around the giant cloister in pursuit of an inflated pig's bladder or equivalent football substitute.)

Those two deviations from customary monastic layout and design were necessary because, although they all shared the same site, Carthusians lived as hermits. The cloister had to be very large in order to accommodate the monks' individual cells built around its perimeter, in essence creating a whole series of miniature monasteries. As the Carthusian doctrine centred on time spent in private prayer and devotion, a vast church for collective formal worship was unnecessary. Mass was communally celebrated, but without the processional rituals practised by other orders.

Cells were virtually identical and most had their own small enclosed garden, tended by the monks themselves. The term 'cell' might be somewhat misleading as it suggests restricted space and minimal furnishings, but those allocated to the Carthusians resembled small, humble cottages with a living room, a study, a bedroom and a first-floor workroom. The door that led from the cloister was the only access, and immediately next to it was a square recess in the wall, which served as a hatch where lay brothers left food for the occupant without interrupting periods of prayer or meditation. Sundays and major festivals were the only occasions when meals were taken communally in the small refectory, but even then silence was generally observed.

Although the facilities shown in a recently reconstructed cell might appear less Spartan than one might imagine,

the monks still followed a harsh, self-imposed physical and spiritual regime compared to those adopted by other orders. They rigidly adhered to a daily timetable during which the longest period of rest occurred some time between 6 p.m. and 11 p.m. The remaining nineteen hours were punctuated by meditation, privately recited offices, manual labour, church worship and a further short rest in the early hours, sandwiched between matins and prime. The only two meals of the day were taken at around 10 a.m. and 4 p.m.; what amounted to fasting was considered essential by Carthusians, who believed that poverty of the body increased spiritual wealth.

Provision of fresh water to each cell for drinking and ablutions required considerably more plumbing than in an establishment where such facilities were centralized for general use. Fortunately, Mount Grace's location directly beneath the steep-sided Hambleton Hills ensured a ready supply from several springs, each capped with its own small, stone-built well house and piped throughout the site.

Unlike other orders, whose numbers gradually declined as enthusiasm for monastic life waned, the Carthusian movement's intense spirituality continued to attract aspiring candidates right up to the Dissolution. Mount Grace itself even had a waiting list during the early sixteenth century.

Photographing Abbeys and Monasteries

OMPILING THIS BOOK has certainly been a challenge, not simply of logistics but of trying to be in the right place at the right time to capture each and every church or abbey ruin in the best possible light. This feat was not made any easier by working through the meteorological mayhem of summer 1998 – a bizarre combination of southern heat haze and northern deluge!

A brief glimpse at the map on page 17 will give some indication of the distances involved, and although a large proportion of the sites are conveniently located in my half of Britain (unfortunately also the wet half), other regions are equally well represented. The Midlands and Home Counties, however, seem sadly devoid of photogenic sites, as close proximity to larger centres of population made them more susceptible to total demolition for their valuable materials.

I have tried to create a harmonious balance between interior and exterior images as well as to focus on some of the more intricate details of craftsmanship that contribute so much to the character and appeal of our churches, so easily overlooked when they are hidden away in gloomy recesses.

Stone buildings can be photographed at any time but they undoubtedly benefit from strong directional light to accentuate every carved detail and the subtle nuances of texture. Early morning or late afternoon sunshine gives additional warmth and colour to limestone churches. At these times the sun's low angle casts shadows that not only create additional atmosphere but also throw important aspects of a building into sharp relief.

I used an Olympus camera and found my 35 mm perspective control lens invaluable in ensuring that walls, towers and pillars retained their vertical lines. Fuji Velvia 50 ASA slide film is outstanding for its depth of colour and quality of reproduction, and despite its slow speed, I would not dream of using anything else.

There is obviously a large selection of books available for further reading on the subject of abbeys and monasteries, and English Heritage and most cathedrals have excellent bookshops offering titles ranging from basic guides for the casual visitor through to serious architectural histories.